**W9-AMI-458**

"Kim Maxwell's *Career Diary of a Fashion Stylist* is an informative, yet fun book. It's comprehensive and will appeal to a variety of entrepreneurs who are ready to burst into the fashion industry. Day-to-day responsibilities and lessons learned help one to conceive how important it is to remain positive and composed. Professionalism and determination are key. With those two, success isn't far behind."
—Erica James, President/CEO of Profetik, LLC

"Simply put, *Career Diary of a Fashion Stylist* is truly a breath of fresh air. Kim Maxwell's perspective provides a telling peak into the goings-on of the fashion industry in both an honest and informative manner. Kudos to Maxwell for a job well done."
—DeWayne J. Rogers, journalist and author of *The Fly Guy Chronicles*

"An excellent book for aspiring stylists as well as more experienced ones. *Career Diary of a Fashion Stylist* is a must-have for all fashion stylists! The book explains the good, the bad, and the ugly of this highly popular career. Bravo to Kim Maxwell for creating a book with so much detail, inspiration, and preparation. One thing's for sure, this book has found a new home in my fashion styling institution."
—Keyonna S.Cox, CEO, House of Style

"*Career Diary of a Fashion Stylist* is a spot-on depiction of the highs and lows of the ever hectic life of a fashion stylist. Kim Maxwell gives an enlightening recount of a profession that many pursue, but even fewer survive. It's an essential part of every stylist's kit!"
—Mychael Knight, fashion designer and stylist

CAREER DIARY™

OF A

FASHION
STYLIST

*Thirty days behind the scenes
with a professional.*

GARDNER'S CAREER DIARIES™

KIM MAXWELL

GARTH GARDNER COMPANY

GGC publishing

Washington DC, USA · London, UK

Cover Photography courtesy: Drexina Nelson/Drexina Nelson
Photography

Editorial inquiries concerning this book should be mailed to: The Editor,
Garth Gardner Company, 5107 13th Street N.W., Washington DC 20011
or emailed to: info@ggcinc.com.http://www.gogardner.com

ISBN-13: 978-1-58965-038-1

Library of Congress Cataloging-in-Publication Data

Maxwell, Kim.
Career diary of a fashion stylist: thirty days behind the scenes with a
professional: Gardner's career diaries / Kim Maxwell.
    p. cm.

    ISBN-13: 978-1-58965-038-1

1. Fashion—United States—Vocational guidance. 2. Clothing trade—
United States—Vocational guidance. 3. Maxwell, Kim—Diaries. I. Garth
Gardner Company. II. Title.

TT507.M38 2007

746.9'2023--dc22

                                    2007047016

Printed in Canada

TABLE OF CONTENTS

Photo by Treagen K. Colston/Treagenphotography.com

ACKNOWLEDGMENTS

I wish to thank GOD, all my friends, and family members who have supported and encouraged me down through the years. To my parents, Felix and Teresa Maxwell—you truly inspire me. To my brother Roderick, my sister Shameka, the Dawson family, the Maxwell family, and my cousins Ladon and Quarn—you've always been there for me. To Christa Jackson of Phenom Marketing & Media—thanks for believing in me, you have truly been a good friend and an angel. I'm extremely grateful to my assistant, Lakeisha Massey. Much appreciation goes out to my long list of friends: Erica James; Laffany Sullivan; Amyr Heard; Keja Jones; Desmond., Kimberly and Dallas Webster; Montrell Dobbins; LaTanya Quinn; Dionne Wynn; Quincy Young; Darren Miller; Tameka Gordon; Felicia Samuels; Rudolph Horner; Pauletta Russell; and Touré Douzart. Thanks to my colleagues in the industry, Mychael Knight and Keshia Walker. Last but hardly least, I'd like to express my gratitude to all my clients who have booked STYLESbyMAXX in the past, as well as those yet to come.

BIOGRAPHY

My name is Kim Maxwell and I'm a fashion stylist, personal shopper and image consultant. I've been involved in the fashion industry for nine years, having worked with record labels that include Sony, Universal, and BME, modeling agencies such as Elite, celebrities Michelle Kwan, Jagged Edge, and Daron (Group 112), and magazines that include Women's Health & Fitness. I've also been a personal shopper and fashion consultant for several clients including Playtex and Hanes, and I've worked as a wardrobe stylist in advertising, promotions, and on commercials featuring Def Jam Recordings, Apple Bottoms/Pimp Juice, and NASCAR. I've also been involved with such television shows as ABC's Are You Hot, and Women's Entertainment Television's wedding show, Get Married.

Born and raised in Tennessee, I've studied fashion since I was a teenager. I always wanted to work in the industry, having taken fashion-merchandising classes in high school. Those classes and my fascination with fashion magazines sparked my interest in learning more about working in the industry. I graduated from Middle Tennessee State University with a bachelor's degree in fashion merchandising and minors in marketing and advertising. After that I decided being a celebrity fashion stylist and image consultant was the career for me. I wanted to be that person behind the scenes who coordinates wardrobe for magazine photo spreads, recording artists, actors and actresses, thereby creating looks for the whole world to see.

My quest began in Nashville. It's the country music, not the fashion capital of the world, so I had to devise a plan to accumulate experience and build my resume. I got started by contacting modeling agencies all around town to see if an internship was available. Not only did I wish to learn how to run a fashion business, but I also wanted a chance to style the wardrobe for the comp cards and portfolios the models needed. The Hurd Modeling Agency & Troupe took me on as an intern, and I also worked as a part-time salesperson and assistant visual merchandiser for a clothing retailer, Wet Seal. There I helped coordinate wardrobe selections for the store-window displays and advised customers on optimal fashion choices. At Hurd I learned the ins and outs of running an agency and booking gigs for models. Once I had gone as far as I could working for someone else, I left the agency and started my own business, STYLESbyMAXX. I do image consulting for artists or individuals who are anxious to find a new look, and my overall style can be described in one word—jazzy. It's my aim to make my clients feel comfortable in their clothes and with how they appear in public. In this industry, after all, "image is everything."

In the beginning I did plenty of research networking with Nashville-area photographers and makeup artists, where we collaborated on test photo shoots. It was a great way to get my foot in the door, since everyone needed high-quality pictures and each of us brought something special to the mix. I was building a strong following, but I knew my career would only move to next level if I changed markets. I needed to find a place that would not only allow me to improve my portfolio, but also provide me with a steady stream of clients. I tried Los Angeles a couple of times, but a short visit to Atlanta yielded almost immediate results in networking and solid booking opportunities. The city and I were an ideal fit.

Since then I've built a strong foundation for my company, and my name is really well-known. It has been a long and stressful journey, but also fun and highly rewarding. The things I've learned by trial and error, and all the risks I've taken, have ultimately made me a stronger businesswoman. Everything has come together for me in Atlanta—my education, the learning experiences I enjoyed as an intern at The Hurd Agency, all those hours of researching a career in fashion styling, and working on hundreds of photo shoots. Because of all that, I've built up my wardrobe contacts, created a dynamite portfolio, and own an enviable client list. I can't say that this is my final stop in the world of fashion styling, but it's pretty clear, STYLESbyMAXX is a great starting place.

CURRENT POSITION AND RESPONSIBILITIES

As a fashion stylist and personal shopper, my role is to acquire and coordinate wardrobes for personal appearances, photo shoots, television shows, and other kinds of public performances. When working in television my position is known as wardrobe stylist. I'm also an image consultant, for which I formulate specific an image for a professional entertainer.

I'm responsible for staying current on fashion trends, so I spend a huge amount of time doing research. I see what new collections are in designer showrooms, boutiques, and department stores, as well as what is happening in "street fashion." Working with a client starts off with a consultation, during which I find out about their likes and dislikes. I also focus on what they are trying to achieve and how they want to be perceived by the public and their fans. We discuss budget, including how much they plan on spending to accomplish their look.

My fashion and image-consulting agency, STYLESbyMAXX, has a variety of components. A booking agent helps me generate jobs, negotiate contracts, and collect fees from clients. My agent also serves as my publicist, sending out information to various media outlets to generate "buzz" on my behalf. My assistant does everything from pulling wardrobe for a photo shoot to taping shoes. I couldn't run my company successfully without having these two people in my corner. I spend much of my time online, researching designer collections and checking my continuous stream of

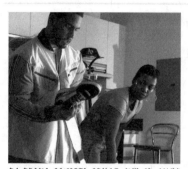

DJ DRAMA GANGSTA GRILLZ MIX CD COVER
SHOOT. PHOTO BY DESMOND TUCKERSON

e-mails—my link to the world of fashion and fame.
My job involves much more than being a nine-to-five
profession. As a freelancer, I'm responsible for generating
my own work. As a result, there are truly no holidays and no
set schedule. Being a fashion stylist is fun, but it's hard work.
You spend a great deal of time publicizing yourself and
building a decent portfolio before any well-paying jobs come
your way. When I first started out as a stylist, I did plenty of
jobs for free just to gain experience. But after building up
my book and the substantial client base that went with it,
the sky became the limit when it came to earning money
and hobnobbing with the rich and famous.

RESUME

Position: Fashion stylist, image consultant and personal shopper

MOVIE PREMIERE
Fighting Temptations movie premiere (actor/comedian Rickey Smiley)

TELEVISION
Are You Hot [ABC], (contestant Raquel Riley)
Honeys [UPN pilot]
Hotlanta Nights
Just Fab Network
The Undiscovered [Travel Channel], (contestant Kerri Ann)
Urban Makeovers: Diamonds in a Ruff [National Film & Video]
Get Married Television [Women's Entertainment Television/ Life Time Channel]

EDITORIAL
Black Men magazine
Cover
Do!
Industry Status Magazine (fashion editor)
Women's Health & Fitness

RECORDING ARTISTS & OTHER CELEBRITIES
Bohagon
Daron (Group 112)
Divinity

DJ Drama
GRITS
Jagged Edge
Bad Gryl
Michelle Kwan

MUSIC VIDEOS
Hotep
Real Deal Records
Remi & Young'n
YZ

PRINT ADS, COMMERCIALS & PROMOTIONS
AppleBottoms/Pimp Juice
Def Jam Recordings
Gangsta Grillz MixTape Series
Hanes
Just My Size
NASCAR
Playtex
Sony Music
Tiger Beer

RETAILERS
Wet Seal

MODELING AGENCIES
Click
Elite
Karin Models

Next
Spectrum Management

PHOTOGRAPHERS
Daniel Acres
Christian Behr
Derek Blanks
Shawn Dowell
Jim Hancock
Christopher Huber
Prince/Atlanta Royal
Ben Rose
Seth Sabal
Chris Standford
Bo Streeter
Paul Thatcher
Marie Thomas
Desmond Tuckerson
Zach Wolfe

EDUCATION
Middle Tennessee State University (Murfreesboro), B.S.
Fashion Merchandising

Day 1 | *JANUARY 2*

PREDICTIONS
- *Confirm tomorrow's meeting with a marketing company and a fashion designer*
- *Follow up with a West Coast-based actor's rep*
- *Check e-mails and revise my MySpace page*
- *Contact a TV show's wardrobe manager*

DIARY

I'm expecting this to be a big year for me, since I already have some serious projects in the works. Today is a catch-up day, where I'm concentrating on office duties. I begin by reviewing my to-do list, which helps me stay organized. Tomorrow I'm meeting with Keshia Walker—president of Insights Marketing and Promotion—and Mychael Knight, the fashion designer from the television show Project Runway. Insights is based right here in Atlanta. I'm taking on the role of go-between, making wardrobe selections for a celebrity pool party being promoted on behalf of a major liquor distiller. Even though I'm not actually styling the wardrobe, it's an opportunity to build a business relationship with the marketing people as well as the beverage company. They'll need a total of twenty swimsuits. I selected the fashion designer for this event because I only coordinate and style wardrobe items rather than design them. Mych and I have worked together for several years, so I'm excited to have him on my team for this project.

Tomorrow is our initial pre-production meeting. Since

I'm coordinating the wardrobe, I'll be responsible for setting up this meeting of the minds. The president of the marketing company has requested specific items from the fashion designer before we start the project. I'll need to make sure Mych remembers they're due tomorrow. In the entertainment and fashion industry, as with any field these days, most communicating is done electronically. I spend close to half of every day reading and sending e-mails from my Sidekick, which is a brand of PDA. I e-mail Keshia and Mych to confirm the time, date and place of our meeting. I also remind Mych that the marketing company is expecting fabric samples and designer sketches, as well as a written timeline and cost estimates.

However, I discover there's a small problem. Mych tells me the PMS colors the client wants for the swimsuits are used only in print material, and he'll actually need the Pantone colors for textiles. PMS colors and Pantones are essentially color palettes. The designer wants me to find the equivalent of their desired PMS color in the Pantone system. I'm hopeful the marketing company has access to that information, but I guess we'll know more about that tomorrow.

Meanwhile I'm multi-tasking by checking messages sent to my personal e-mail account and MySpace Web site. Checking e-mail is an all-day task for me, one that rarely stops before I go to bed. I haven't checked the MySpace messages in four days, so it takes me a couple of hours to do so and to revise my corporate page. MySpace has proven to be a terrific marketing and networking tool for my company, STYLESbyMAXX.

Then it's time for my daily conference call with my booking agent, Christa Jackson. She is responsible for finding and booking jobs for me, as well as negotiating fees, collecting payments, and sending out my portfolio to potential clients. For those services I pay her anywhere from fifteen to twenty percent of whatever I earn on the jobs she confirms. Our daily call is where we discuss what projects we have that day or coming up in the near future. Having a booking agent allows me to focus on being creative, while she looks after the business side of things. It's also good to have someone else do the negotiating, since I'm inclined to take it personally whenever potential clients want to low-ball my rates. Christa takes the strain off me, and she's really good when it comes to haggling with potential clients over money.

I ask Christa to follow up with a potential client who contacted us prior to Christmas. They're an agency that represents the actor, Jermaine Williams, who is based in Los Angeles. He has been in the movies Fat Albert, Stomp the Yard, The Comebacks and the television show, Veronica Mars. Jermaine has a movie premiere coming up later in January. Last month Christa sent over all the information they requested, but there's been no reply so far; meanwhile, the movie opens in six days. Christa tells me she left the actor's rep a message and is waiting for a return call.

After that I call the head of the makeup, wardrobe and hair

department for the *Get Married* TV show. I've been hired as their wardrobe stylist for the next thirteen episodes that will air on WE—Women's Entertainment Television. I leave her a voice-mail message to call me, since I need to see what's going on with the show before I start preparing for it. This will be my first national TV show, and I want to make sure I give it my full attention. I also check with a publicist who contacted me about styling a fashion show for a children's charitable foundation. I'll be responsible for providing wardrobe choices for close to a hundred children. I sent over a budget request several weeks ago, but so far it's gone unanswered.

By the end of the day I'm still waiting for return phone calls from the actor's rep, the TV wardrobe manager, and several other potential clients. I've spent considerable time on the computer today, but my e-mails are caught up and I'm ready to prepare for tomorrow's meeting.

LESSONS/PROBLEMS

The issues I dealt with today reflect the variety of functions I perform, such as securing Pantone colors for the designer and making sure I have enough time to pull off this movie premiere. It's also important to start prepping for the *Get Married* show. We begin taping in mid-January, and I want to feel I have everything under control.

Day 2 | JANUARY 3

PREDICTIONS
- Meet with a marketing person and a fashion designer
- Meet with my booking agent

DIARY
Our marketing meeting takes place at a local coffee shop. Because I work from home, it's more professional if I meet clients in a public place or at their office. This get-together with the marketing president and the fashion designer goes well, with solid agreement all around on the creative direction we're taking. Mych brings along his Pantone book so we can review color samples. He shows us sketches he has made of the swimsuit designs, and they look great! Keshia seems especially pleased with them.

Since we're experiencing difficulties in locating the proper hues, the marketing folks will have their client overnight the PMS color scheme they're using so Mych can match them as closely as possible. The marketing company and the client have asked for five different swimsuit designs in five separate colors, each one representing the different liquors they make. Keshia has brought the bottles of liquor with her, which gives us a chance to see exactly what colors they want. We peer closely at the bottles and match them as best we can to the colors in the Pantone book.

I help Keshia pick out the designs I think will look best for this event, while Mych suggests what colors will look great

MEETING WITH KESHIA WALKER, PRESIDENT OF INSIGHTS MARKETING AND PROMOTION AND FASHION DESIGNER, MYCHAEL KNIGHT.

with each of the five designs. Because everyone came fully prepared to this meeting, the project is off to a fast start. Keshia announces the swimsuits will be used for a celebrity pool party sponsored by their client, scheduled to take place during Super Bowl weekend in Miami. The party itself will be at the Versace Mansion. I'm impressed with the knowledge that one of my projects will involve the world-famous fashion designer, Gianna Versace. She plans to host several events throughout the weekend that will feature these swimsuits.

I present my client with an invoice and she writes me a check as a deposit. Before the meeting ends we discuss overall costs and timelines for having the swimsuits produced. We agree on a deadline that will put them in the marketing company's hands no later than a week before the event. I'm excited because I've added a new client to my list, which is what makes my business grow. The next step is to have the marketing company's client approve the swimsuits. Mych will overnight his color sketches to the liquor company, and I'll stay on top of things until the project is wrapped up.

Afterwards I meet with my booking agent, who tells me the actor's rep has finally called her back. Apparently they're working with a limited budget, which is fine with me because I'm anxious to build this particular relationship. Christa explains we're no longer discussing next week's premiere, but instead we'll do one for a movie he has coming out in March. She'll set up a conference call a few days from now that will include me, the actor, and his representatives. When I return to my office I check my e-mails and leave another message for the wardrobe head at Get Married. I sure hope she calls back tomorrow.

LESSONS/PROBLEMS
The difficulty I had in finding the proper colors for the swimsuits was resolved when the designer brought along a Pantone book. We used that information to figure out which shades the client wanted, and we'll be able to match them to everyone's satisfaction. I can't wait to see how these swimsuits turn out.

PREDICTIONS

- *Speak with my booking agent*
- *Pick up a check from my marketing client*
- *Deliver swimsuit sketches by e-mail and in person*

DIARY

My workday begins with a nine o'clock call to my booking agent. Christa tells me a publicist for a Michigan-based hip-hop group is interested in hiring me to style their five members. A publicist is generally responsible for molding an artist's image, which includes arranging photo shoots for promotional material placed on Web sites and provided to media outlets. Because they're not signed to a major record label, their wardrobe budget is fairly small, only around $3000. That money will have to suffice for both my fee as well as covering the cost of the clothes. The publicist wants two full wardrobe changes, which means I'll be coordinating at least ten outfits. It will actually turn out to be more, since I'll require additional clothes in case something doesn't fit or the client doesn't care for a particular item. I agree to take on the assignment because I'm anxious to expand my influence in this area. While they may not be an important hip-hop group today, they could be in the future. Even on a tight budget I'm confident I can pull it off, so I instruct Christa to move forward. Later the group's publicist will confirm a meeting time with the singers, their road manager, and the rest of their creative team, which consists of a photographer and one assistant.

SKETCHES OF THE SWIMSUITS THAT MYCHAEL KNIGHT DESIGNED FOR THE INSIGHTS MARKETING PROJECT.

Christa also reports we have a conference call scheduled with the movie actor and his management people at one o'clock tomorrow. We'll use that call to make some basic introductions and outline my experience as a stylist. I'll also provide ideas as to how I see him appearing when it comes to wardrobe and an overall look. I do some Web research, checking out his online bio and viewing the way his agency portrays his image. That gives me some ideas of what I think will work, and I add a few unique twists that should make them sit up and take notice.

As soon as I get off the phone, the president of the marketing company tells me she needs two printed-out color copies of the swimsuit sketches immediately—one for herself and one for her client's review. She needs them electronically as well. We're in a hurry because she has a plane to catch, and this material has to be on that flight with her. That means she must get them no later than five o'clock. However, the designer is currently working on a different project and can't sneak away to have color copies made. On top of that he doesn't have a digital scanner, so there's no way he can e-mail the sketches anywhere. It's up to me to step in and make this happen. Mych will also require a deposit before he's willing to let go of the work.

I agree to pick up a check for him from the marketing company, which will allow him to release the sketches to me. Then I'll take the art to be color-copied and scanned. We're having some wild weather today, with tornado warnings in effect and a really strong rainstorm moving through the city. Even though it's pouring, I have to get out there and do what's expected of me. I want to make sure my marketing client gets whatever she needs so she can get the designs to the liquor company for approval. After all, what I'm offering is a service, and one of my main goals is to make sure the client stays happy. I run around the city while it rains so heavily I can barely see well enough to drive. My first stop is at an office supply store to get the color copies made, and then I visit a colleague's office to use her scanner. I scan the sketches and save the file to a portable drive before heading over to Keshia's office. There I hand her assistant one set of sketches to be shipped overnight to the liquor company. The extra copy is for her boss. I also e-mail the sketches so they can be downloaded onto her desktop when she returns from her trip. Once I'm back in my home office, I follow up with an e-mail to let Keshia know the check was picked up, copies of the sketches were left at her office as well as transmitted electronically, and that one set is on its way to her client. I'm sure she's pleased her deadline was met.

LESSONS/PROBLEMS

No matter whether it's rainy or sunny, deadlines are written in stone. Because mine is a service business, at the end of the day it's all about making my client happy and providing whatever they need to complete the project at hand. I used my brains and my networking connections to solve the problems I encountered today, such as not owning a scanner.

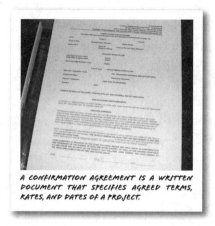

A CONFIRMATION AGREEMENT IS A WRITTEN DOCUMENT THAT SPECIFIES AGREED TERMS, RATES, AND DATES OF A PROJECT.

Day 4 | JANUARY 6

PREDICTIONS

- *Hold a conference call with the actor and his management team*
- *Meet in person with the hip-hop group and their entourage*

DIARY

All that running around yesterday left me exhausted. But it's a new day with new possibilities, so I look forward to moving ahead. I start at noon in anticipation of my one o'clock conference call. Preparations include looking over the file I compiled on the actor, who I hope we can turn into a client. This material consists of his official biography, e-mails from the actor's management team that outline his upcoming projects, and the wardrobe concepts I created for him yesterday. It's important that I'm fully prepared for this meeting. First impressions are everything in this business, and I really want to land this client.

When the time comes, Christa calls me and we conference in the movie actor and his associates. We break the ice by discussing some of the fun things we like to do in our spare time. I explain the way I operate as a stylist and mention the wardrobe ideas I came up with yesterday, which are well received. The actor says he'll be in Atlanta sometime over the next couple of months, and we'll be able to meet face-to-face at that time. Everyone seems to be on the same page as far as the actor's image is concerned, and I'm sure we'll work well together.

After we're finished, Christa stays on the line to tell me the hip-hop group and their publicist want to meet us at five o'clock to discuss their photo shoot. We agree that I'll show them samples of my work, discuss our expectations for the shoot, and then do an overall consultation on their image. Then we'll sign a confirmation agreement and receive a check as a deposit to cover up-front expenses. Christa invites me to her office so we can work on the budget and draw up the agreement.

The group's total budget is $3000. Since this is a fairly small amount of money, especially with five guys and two wardrobe changes each, the clothes will have to be rented. Working on the assumption that this shoot will take two days, my day rate for this assignment works out to $1500. My agent is entitled to twenty percent of that, plus I'll charge a $250 kit fee for parking, gas, and other elements I need to successfully style the shoot. That includes everything from paying my assistant to leasing wardrobe racks and buying shoe polish, tape, pens, lint brushes, and numerous other items. The remaining balance will go toward wardrobe rental fees and miscellaneous expenses. Christa and I agree this is a workable budget, if perhaps a bit tight, so she calls up the publicist to find out the group's record label information for inclusion in the agreement. As a stylist, your rate will always be contingent on whatever budget the client has allocated for the project. You have to decide if you can work within that budget. I've seen day rates range from $250 a day to $10,000 a day. Because of my significant experience, I can easily charge anywhere from $1500 to $3500 a day.

We print out the agreement just in time to leave for the meeting. Everyone will be there—all five performers, their manager, the group's publicist, and their creative team. Whenever I'm setting up an artist's consultation, I prefer to get the whole team involved. With all five singers on hand, I'll be able to judge each guy's personality on a face-to-face basis, which is the best way to do it. I open the meeting with a slide show of my past work, which is well received by everyone. Next we brainstorm the sort of image we want to project during the photo shoot. A number of solid ideas come out of this session, with just about everyone contributing something worthwhile. We arrive at a mutually acceptable date for the shoot—next Wednesday at noon— and agree to come up with a location at a later time. Then I sit down with each artist, quizzing them on what size clothes they wear, what they like or dislike about specific wardrobe items, and how they see themselves from a clothing image standpoint. This consultation goes smoothly, and I'm pleased to discover that we all have similar thoughts about the direction of their wardrobe. I also take pictures so I'll be able to refer to individual photos while I'm selecting wardrobe items for each of the five artists. While I'm involved with the performers, my booking agent is reviewing the confirmation agreement with their management team. The terms are fine and the budget is approved, so everyone signs on the dotted line and a check changes hands. I provide their manager with a receipt, and we're pretty much set to go. I have four or five days to pull everything together, which should be plenty of time.

On my way home I stop by a bookstore and pick up some hip-hop magazines to help provide inspiration. These magazines are perfect research tools, showing off the sort of outfits other artists in the genre are wearing. It's important that my clients stand out from everyone else in the industry. By ten o'clock I'm ready for bed. Over the next couple of days I'll begin the planning for this photo shoot.

LESSONS/PROBLEMS
Once again I've proven to myself that organization and preparation are the keys to running a successful consultation. Internal organization is just as important, especially since I have multiple projects going on at the same time. This is the first time I'll have worked with such a large group. I'm

a bit nervous about that, but if I stay organized and think every step through, I'll be fine.

Day 5 | JANUARY 7

PREDICTIONS

- Start a file folder for the hip-hop group
- Set up a conference call with my assistant
- Work on creating a wardrobe image for the hip-hop group

DIARY

After returning home from church I decide to create a file for the hip-hop group's photo shoot. When creating such a file, I make sure I have all the information I need about the artist and the project under consideration. This type of client file helps me stay organized. It contains a signed confirmation agreement between my company and the client, an envelope where I keep all the receipts for such expenditures as wardrobe and accessories, a tearsheet of personal information, a copy of the artist's CD—if the client is a musician—plus contact information for all parties and an artist's information sheet. The more organized I am, the easier it is for me to stay on top of things.

The client confirmation agreement is a document that describes our professional relationship, such as booking information, rates, terms, conditions, the wardrobe addendum, and how I'll be credited on the photo shoot. Having the artist's CD on hand is important, because I need to be familiar with his or her's music in order to understand what sort of look I want to create for the shoot. Contact information is critical, including everyone's telephone number and e-mail address. If I have questions regarding the shoot, I'll need to know how to reach the appropriate people, especially regarding details of wardrobe, budget or invoicing. The tearsheet outlines the artist's likes and dislikes and serves to remind me of the specific style we're going for. I also make note of the artist's measurements, the number of members in the group and everyone's ages, the name and contact details for the photographer or the director, how many looks we're doing, and anything else I'm afraid I'll forget if it isn't written down.

After putting everything together I speak at length on the phone with my assistant, Lakeisha. She's been my assistant for two years. I was motivated to hire her because of her passion for the business, and she's continued to work for me because she's equally enthusiastic about her goals and the job she does. She's trustworthy and offers excellent suggestions, so we make a good team. Whenever I'm working on a major project, or more than one at a time, I really need someone to help me put everything together. For this particular shoot Lakeisha will assist in selecting the wardrobe and prep the clothes for the shoot, and she'll also remain on scene to help out with the styling. Finally, she'll return the wardrobe items to their respective suppliers once the shoot is over. One of our topics for conversation today is her rate of pay. Her day rate can range from between $100 to $500, depending on the budget we've worked out with the client. In this case I'll be paying her $100. There are times when the budget is too tight to allow money for an assistant, at which point she has to decide if it's worth working on the project simply for the experience. Today we discuss our expectations for the photo shoot and the image the client and I wish to portray. I ask for her schedule so I can plan how best to use her time when we do our shopping.

I flip through the hip-hop magazines I picked up at the bookstore. My research technique involves reviewing magazines that best fit the image we're trying to create for the client. This research is a very important part of getting the job done correctly. Not only do I use magazines as a tool and a reference guide when consulting with the client, but also in preparation for the shoot itself. For this photo shoot, I look through all entertainment, hip-hop and music-related publications. I'm specifically checking out display ads inserted by urban wear designers. I also look to see which fashion trends are popular in hip-hop, as well as what I can do to make my client stand out from the rest of the crowd. As a stylist, my goal is to make sure my client's image reflects the hip-hop market. I finish up with a brainstorming session to select the most creative look I can find. It seems best to play off the street image each individual artist requested at our meeting, but I also want to incorporate a crisp, mature, and fashionable edge.

LESSONS/PROBLEMS

If I'm going to be successful with this hip-hop photo shoot, I'll need to have my assistant involved all along the way. It's a complex project, especially because I haven't worked with this group before and we've decided on a different style for each artist. I have nothing to use as a reference point, since the group has no prior promotional photos.

What I've designed in my head may be totally different from what they're expecting, but creating a tearsheet validates the fact that we have the same styles in mind. I've listened to this group's CD and am using the information from our consultation to better understand their expectations. All these tools should increase the accuracy with which I help them create the image they want. Of course, I'll know for sure once I get to the shoot, where everyone will see which wardrobe items we've pulled.

MY APPOINTMENT BOOK HELPS ME KEEP TRACK OF MY BUSY SCHEDULE.

Day 6 | *JANUARY 8*

PREDICTIONS

- *Select final images for the hip-hop group*
- *Go shopping for wardrobe items and accessories*
- *Sign a contract and fax it to the TV production company*
- *Check the completeness of my stylist kit*

DIARY

This is my second prep day for the hip-hop group's photo shoot. The lead work involves consulting with the client, doing research to provide artistic inspiration, selecting the shops where the clothes will come from, lining up fittings, and making sure all the clothes are clean and pressed for the actual session. Today I'll try to find just the right boutique or designer showroom that will have what I want in stock. In the middle of checking e-mails and creating my to-do list for the day, my phone rings. It's the president of the hip-hop group's record label, telling me the group's custom-made jewelry will not be ready in time for the shoot. That means I'll need to source something for them, including diamond necklaces and charms, plus wristwatches. This level of bling can easily cost $100,000 or more. With a wardrobe budget of $1250 for five guys, the only way I can add jewelry is to rent it. I review my contact book and start calling all the jewelers listed there, as well as friends in the entertainment industry who might know someone. There's one thing every hip-hop artist needs in a photo shoot, and that's flashy jewelry.

At a coffee shop I go through my files, seeking to solidify the photo concepts we'll use. We're doing two looks for this shoot. The first one will be shot in a warehouse, so the wardrobe should be highly urban, even industrial. The second one will be taken in a boardroom, so the wardrobe needs to involve business-type attire, but with a "street" feel to it. Once I've settled on the proper styling for each performer's body type, it's time to hit the malls to see what's new. For this project I've decided on USA Boutique, one of the hottest urban designer shops in Atlanta. I'll try their store at South Dekalb Mall first. On the way I receive a call from a friend of mine who had checked with a jeweler on my behalf. The owner turned us down because he didn't want to risk having that much jewelry out, even though we'll be paying for a security detail.

With everything else going on, I barely remember to fax my wardrobe contract over to the *Get Married* TV production office. This is a wedding program airing on the Women's Entertainment Channel, and I've been hired to style the show's two hosts. Because the clothes will be rented or sponsored, I'll need to make sure the wardrobe is secured. Under the terms of our agreement, I'm the one responsible for the wardrobe while it's out.

On my way to South Dekalb Mall I get a phone call from another jeweler. He designs custom jewelry and has nothing in stock right now, although he might be able to obtain what we need from one of his vendors. I describe what we want and ask him to estimate the cost to rent it. In these cases he charges by the hour rather than by the piece, and I'll also need to hire a security detail since we're talking about some very expensive items. Because we'll need the jewelry on the set for at least four hours, I figure it will cost more than a thousand dollars to rent it. After getting the client's approval to add this cost to the budget, I tell the jeweler to make the necessary arrangements. Then Keshia checks in to tell me her liquor client has approved the swimsuit sketches, which means we can move forward to get them designed.

At USA Boutique's South Dekalb Mall store, even though it's clear they have exactly what we need, I soon realize we'll need to obtain additional wardrobe items. The number is probably closer to fifteen looks than ten. And even though I'm renting the wardrobe, I don't want to take their entire inventory. The manager suggests we can draw from their downtown location, which is a big help. After checking out the rest of the mall shops for future hip-hop wardrobe opportunities, it's time for lunch and then a cruise downtown to retrieve the rest of my USA Boutique outfits.

After that I head over to Lenox Mall, where I trade a deposit check to the jeweler for a copy of the invoice. This is some seriously expensive stuff—$80,000 for the necklaces, $11,000 for the charms, and $37,000 for the watches. Lenox Mall is an upscale place, but checking the various boutiques and department stores yields nothing worthwhile. I'm not all that disappointed, since USA Boutique had everything I needed.

It's nine o'clock by the time I finally make it home, but I still have to check over my stylist kit. Having an organized kit is important because these are items I need for every shoot to make the wardrobe look better. I stock double-sided tape, lint brushes, safety pins, several different shoe polish colors, garment racks, a sewing needle and thread, scissors, a clothes steamer, an iron and ironing board, spray starch, and garment bags and hangers. I'm short a few things, so I run to the store to restock before going to bed.

LESSONS/PROBLEMS

Today was a long one, but a photo shoot is very preparation-intensive. My client called with an unexpected request for jewelry without the necessary budget to cover it. There are times when a client has to choose between increasing the budget or doing without something. Fortunately, my client was willing to pay more to do the job correctly. It was also a good thing I planned to go to other stores rather than focusing on just a single showroom or boutique.

Day 7 | JANUARY 9

PREDICTIONS
- Meet with my assistant, Lakeisha, to pull wardrobe items
- Pick up additional items at stores around town
- Prepare wardrobe items for the shoot

DIARY
Today is the final day before the hip-hop shoot. I'm set to meet Lakeisha at ten o'clock at USA Boutique's South Dekalb Mall store, where we'll pick up most of the wardrobe items we'll need. I use each artist's fact sheet as a guide to pull the proper items. It's important for outfits to portray the proper individual image as well as flow well with everyone else in the group. There should be a sense of balance in these group shots, although that doesn't mean everyone should wear the same clothes. One of our artists will be shot in a college-prep look that has some "street" to it, but I'm having a tough time finding the right items. I believe a chocolate-brown bubble vest would go nicely with the polo shirt I've already pulled, plus a bright-colored cashmere sweater in yellow or orange. We'll also need white, yellow and red t-shirts, but this store has none I like. I send Lakeisha out into the mall to find something appropriate while I stay behind at USA Boutique. I finish pulling one complete look for each artist, plus most of the shoes they'll need. Everything else, including the second full look for each artist, will probably come from the chain's downtown location. The sales associate has me sign the wardrobe rental agreement, and I'm on my way out the door.

Lakeisha and I meet up in the middle of the mall and search together for hats, sneakers, and whatever else we might need. She has found the t-shirts but couldn't get either the cashmere sweater or the vest. We happen to pop into a store called Fame, and they have a vest in the right color and size, and for the right price. I snatch it up immediately. Then we discover the perfect sweater at Sports Profile, except it costs more than I'm willing to spend. However, I manage to talk the manager into giving me a better price, so we're both happy with the outcome. Our final stop at this mall is J's Hats, where I find several styles that will work well for the shoot, plus a couple of handkerchiefs I'll work in somehow. By now it's close to one o'clock. In addition to working as my assistant Lakeisha has another part-time job, and she needs to be there in a little more than an hour. But she shows her dedication and offers to meet me downtown to finish up our wardrobe search.

At USA Boutique's downtown store, the selection is even better. We have no problem finishing up the second look, but the clock is ticking. After the manager checks over our wardrobe selections, I sign the rental agreement and load everything into my car. After stopping by my office to drop everything off, I'm on my way to the next stop, Greenbriar Mall. I'd forgotten this mall yesterday, but they have some of the best sneaker stores in the city. I pick up several hats but ironically no sneakers, since nothing special catches my eye. Next is Atlantic Station, where I spot some terrific outfits for me but nothing for the photo shoot. I try not to shop for myself when I'm out working, but it's a hard habit to break. I stay focused on the task at hand and leave Atlantic Station.

My last stop is Lenox Mall, where I pick up sneakers, thermal t-shirts and baseball caps. It's ten o'clock by the time I meet Lakeisha back at my office, and we still have to prepare the wardrobe for tomorrow's shoot. Clothes are stacked everywhere, so we begin by organizing the bags and marking down everything in our possession. I use a two-part sales-order pad to write in, so that I can keep track of what items I have, where they came from, and how much something costs in case the client wants to buy it. When the shoot is over we'll use the same form to log everything back in. I can't afford to misplace even a single item. Lakeisha and I add up our sheets and come out with a wardrobe value of $5400. Added to the jewelry we'll have on the set tomorrow, the total will top $130,000. I feel some anxiety about having that much wardrobe on hand, but everything is insured plus we'll have a security detail in place.

Once each item is logged in, we start to coordinate the wardrobe of each artist in the group. After putting everything together I figure we're short a few items, such as a pair of shoes here or a shirt and jacket there. Because I have such a great relationship with USA Boutique that I know the manager will allow me to go back into the store first thing tomorrow so I can pick up whatever else I need before the shoot.

Preparing clothes for a shoot is a tedious task. While I'm

I USE A RECEIPT BOOK WHEN MY CLIENTS PAY ME IN CASH. MEANWHILE, THE SALES ORDER BOOK IS USED TO LOG-IN WARDROBE.

pulling off the price tags, Lakeisha is steaming the clothes and taping the bottoms of the shoes. Then we sort items by artist and place everything in garment bags, labeling them appropriately so it will be easy to hand off the right outfits to the right artist. Lakeisha and I review our expectations and make sure we know the times and locations. Our shoot begins at noon and should end four hours later.

LESSONS/PROBLEMS

My day ended at three in the morning, and I'll need to be up by eight to get to the store and retrieve the rest of what we'll need for the shoot. It would have helped me today if I owned a larger vehicle, since I could have avoided dropping off part of the wardrobe due to lack of space.

PREDICTIONS

- *Begin the hip-hop photo shoot at noon*
- *Confirm that the jeweler will show up on time*
- *Log in wardrobe items before the shoot starts*

DIARY

When Lakeisha gets to my office at 9:00 A.M., we review the agenda for the shoot today and then pack everything into our cars. We make sure to include our stylist kits as well as all the wardrobe items. Arriving at South Dekalb Mall at ten o'clock, just as it opens, we run into USA Boutique and grab another pair of shoes plus one more shirt-and-jacket combination.

On my way to our first location, The Compound nightclub, the jeweler calls. He tells me he was unable to get all the jewelry we'll need for the shoot because his vendor had previously committed some of the pieces to a trade show at the apparel mart. As a result, he's only bringing about half of what we need for the shoot. I'm quite disturbed by this news, since we truly need all the items I'd requested. He explains he's leaving for the shoot shortly with all the jewelry that he could get from his vendor. I call my client and explain the situation. From his voice it's obvious he's disappointed, but thankfully he's not upset. As a successful business owner, one of my goals is to make sure my client is happy and receives exemplary treatment. Even though the situation is beyond my control, by not supplying what was requested I feel I'm letting my client down. I'll need to figure out what to do with the jewelry once I get to the shoot, because there are five artists and I'll only have half the jewelry I need to complete the looks they've requested.

At The Compound, everything is right on schedule. The photographer and his assistant are setting up for the first shot, and all five artists have arrived along with their management team. Christa is there as well, making sure I have whatever I need to do my job well. She'll also collect the balance of the money from the client once the project is finished. While we wait for the jewelry to arrive, Lakeisha sets up the wardrobe. I pull each artist aside and show him what I've picked out, and everyone seems pleased with his wardrobe selection. Since this is the first time I've worked with this group, I'm relieved by that response.

By half past twelve the jewelry still hasn't shown up, but a quick call to the gentleman informs me he'll be here soon. Before we start, however, the photographer explains that our idea of using two separate locations—the warehouse set and the boardroom set—is out. But because the wardrobe we've pulled together will work regardless of the location, that's not a problem. The difficulty arises when the jeweler walks through the door, accompanied by his security guy. He pulls me aside to deliver some further bad news—he's only able to provide us with two chains! There are no watches or charms, and not even enough chains to go around. Even though I manage to keep my composure, I'm seething inside. After explaining the situation to my client, I can see he's disappointed but we agree to do the best we can under the circumstances. I politely thank the jeweler for coming and explain what I've decided we'll do with such limited inventory. The individual shots are easy, since each artist can take turns wearing the chains. As for the group photos, all we can do is have two of the five guys wear a chain. The jeweler proves more than accommodating, reducing his fee because he didn't bring along all the stuff he promised. He even volunteers to lend us his own diamond ring and bracelet for some of the photos.

After all that, the shoot is easy sailing. The guys look great on camera and everyone has a good time. The photo shoot wraps at four o'clock, right on schedule. Lakeisha logs in every wardrobe item to make sure we won't leave anything behind. One of the artists likes his outfits so much he offers to buy them. My wardrobe suppliers love when this happens. We bag up everything except for these two looks, which he pays for on the spot. Receipts for the wardrobe rentals go to the client, and Christa collects the remaining balance of my day rate. Despite the jewelry glitch, everything turned out well. The client gave me all the tools I needed to make this a successful shoot. The group was fun to work with, and they enjoyed the image I devised and the wardrobe looks I created. I truly look forward to working with them again.

We head back to my office to prepare the clothes to be returned to USA Boutique. We retag the wardrobe items, remove the tape from the soles of the shoes, and check our list one last time to make sure everything is in place.

Because USA Boutique's downtown store is closed by the time we're ready to do the return, we drop everything off at their mall location.

LESSONS/PROBLEMS

Even though the jewelry incident made my day stressful, I kept my composure and handled myself in a professional manner. The fact that my client was willing to be flexible was also a great help. The artists enjoyed the wardrobe I built for them, the photo shoot went smoothly, and everything got returned in good-as-new condition. It's vital that I find additional jewelry suppliers to avoid situations like this in the future.

PREDICTIONS

- *Finish up the hip-hop photo shoot file*
- *Check office e-mails*
- *Take a conference call with my booking agent*

DIARY

I wake up at noon, staying in bed later than usual because the hip-hop photo shoot was so exhausting. I'll take it easy today and concentrate on finishing up my photo shoot paperwork, plus some office work. For the past five days I've been running around, with no time to look at fashion Web sites or catch up on entertainment news, two prime sources of inspiration for me. I'll make sure to do that over the next couple of days, but first I check e-mail and my MySpace page.

I need to wrap up my hip-hop photo shoot file. I create a detailed file for every one of my projects. That allows me to keep up with my clients and all the information that pertains to their particular project. I collect all the receipts and place them in an envelope. Then I make sure the confirmation agreement is in the file. This is a signed document between my client and me that specifies the terms of the project. As with any business, a signed contract is the most important piece of paper you can have. If any disputes arise or confusions ensue, all the terms are right there in black and white. I also include in this file the artist information sheet and the client sheet. In case we work together again, I'll already have this material on hand. Any additional agreements, instructions or promotional material, either regarding the artists themselves or else their management team and publicists, also go into this file. I also file away copies of the wardrobe login sheet so I know which items were used, and where they came from. Now that everything is in order, I can file it away.

Christa, my booking agent, calls me at four o'clock so we can do our project analysis. We always discuss a project after it's over, reviewing what happened and determining if there are things we'd do differently the next time around. We keep the lines of communication open so she knows my likes and dislikes about every project. In the end, this hip-hop photo shoot turned out well. We were pleased that the client acted professionally when negotiating and signing the agreement, and payment was made quickly. We dissected what took place on the set, and I describe to Christa how the jewelry issue stressed me out, but also how we managed to overcome the difficulty and get things moving in the right direction. I tell her I plan to seek out a different jewelry provider for future use, and she agrees it's probably a wise idea. Christa is a wonderful booking agent. We've worked together for two years now, and we really understand what makes the other person tick. I'm impressed that she's always the consummate professional who handles my career with extreme precision.

LESSONS/PROBLEMS
Even though I worked today, I made sure I took it easy.

As my booking agent, Christa is not only a valued team member but also a dear friend. Surrounding yourself with experienced, professional and supportive people is important if you're going to run a successful company. Thankfully there were no difficulties today, because I really needed a break from all that problem solving.

Day 10 | JANUARY 14

PREDICTIONS
- *Work on my self-image*
- *Plan networking trips*

DIARY

My company's slogan is "image is everything." It's important for me to practice what I preach, which means I'll be working on my self-image today. My image is very important because I have to be able to sell my services to potential clients. It's important I look good because I'm a fashion stylist. No one would hire me if I dressed poorly or was in any other way unfashionable. On my agenda today is a new hairstyle, plus I plan to add some key pieces to my wardrobe. In this industry, re-inventing yourself is something you have to do in order to remain marketable and thus successful.

I begin by checking my closet to see what's already on hand. My preferred style is a classic, jazzy and hip look where I incorporate some of the latest fashion trends. If there's anything in my closet I haven't worn in at least a year, it's time to get rid of it. I donate all my unwanted clothes to a local women's shelter. After culling out some older items I make note of the things I'd like to acquire, such as more fitted t-shirts, a cute dress, either black or brown boots, and one or two pairs of jeans. Looking through magazines such as *InStyle* and *Elle* not only inspires me, but it also tells me what I should be adding to my collection. Having some of the hottest new items for the season is crucial if I'm going to stay on top of the fashion game. After making a list I head to the mall. I'll be shopping for some key wardrobe pieces, and it's important to choose just the right store or boutique that reflects my personal style.

Much of my time is spent shopping for other people, so it occasionally feels weird to shop for myself. I do best when I think creatively. I rarely buy clothes right off the mannequin, because that means I'm giving up creative control over my wardrobe and my professional image. There's a risk I'll be dressed exactly like someone else, and that simply shouldn't happen to a fashion expert like me. The way I go about a shopping expedition is very strategic. First I walk into all the stores or boutiques I love and cruise around to see what's on display. I avoid impulse buying because it's important to carefully consider every piece and how it works with clothes already in my closet. Then I'll set a couple of things aside and move on to the next shop. I never buy anything until I've seen what's available in a variety of stores. Even when shopping for myself I remain in a fashion stylist state of mind. After stopping off at all my favorite boutiques I analyze what I've seen and which pieces would look best on me. Today I try on a few things, and then it's time to depart because I have a hair appointment at five o'clock. I've decided to change my hair color. I want something that complements my skin tone and gives me a softer look. I've thought about this step for a long time and even asked my hairstylist for some suggestions. We discuss his advice when I sit down at his station, and suddenly it's time to act.

While I'm in the chair, I have a chance to think about my two upcoming networking trips. Christa and I decided it would be beneficial for us to visit some potential clients outside the Atlanta market. As a freelancer, my top priority is to always seek out more work. We'll visit Los Angeles in the spring and New York City this summer. I've already spoken to several key people over the phone, but there's nothing like a face-to-face meeting to help build a working relationship. I'll do some online research to find airline flights and hotels, and also make a list of the people we'll want to meet. I'll have Christa set everything up, since she's so good at that sort of thing. We'll discuss the list the next time we have a conference call.

Before long my hairstylist is finished, and I'm ready to call it a day. I love the new color we chose, and the style is perfect for the sort of look I want to convey. I'm very excited about the self-image and personal style I created for myself.

LESSONS/PROBLEMS
A person should always invest in themselves and their company. Shopping and getting a new hairstyle is an investment I made for myself and for my self-image. If I look good, then my clients will believe I can make them look good, too.

Day 11 | *JANUARY 15*

PREDICTIONS
- *Work on my corporate MySpace page*
- *Meet with my booking agent*
- *Research various fashion Web sites*

DIARY

I finally have time to put my office in order. Whenever I'm prepping for projects or directly involved in them, my office work gets set aside. I expect the next several weeks will be slow for me, so now's the time to get organized. After all, this is a full-service business I'm running, not merely wardrobe coordination. Office duties can be as exciting as researching the latest fashion trends and designers, and as boring as filing. Although I have an assistant, Lakeisha is most useful to me when she works directly with clients. That also provides her with valuable hands-on experience. I feel I can always take care of the more mundane duties when my projects slow down.

Checking e-mail and reviewing MySpace messages proves to be entertaining rather than tedious. Most of the e-mails are invitations to industry events, or notices of fashion Web site updates, or personal notices of support from friends and family. Since it's a new year, I decide it's time to revise my company's MySpace page. MySpace has proven to be one of my best marketing tools, so it's important for me to keep it fresh and fashionable. I want my page to reflect who I am as a stylist, and what my company is capable of achieving for potential clients. I also add a bit of personal information

MY PRESS KIT PACKAGE WILL INCLUDE MY PRESS KIT FOLDER AND MY COMP CARD. IT WILL BE SENT TO MAGAZINE EDITORS AND POTENTIAL CLIENTS TO GENERATE PUBLICITY AND JOBS.

because I want my page to appear as welcoming as possible. I change the background color scheme, update the company news, and post a photo that shows off my new hairstyle and wardrobe choices. As quickly as I'm posting the updates, I'm already receiving positive feedback from my regular readers. Wow, that was fast! Then I switch my attention to a favorite Web site of mine, Fashion Week Daily. I enjoy reading the postings on this site because they seem to have all the scoops on what's happening in the fashion business—everything from shows to industry gossip.

At three o'clock I arrive at my favorite seafood restaurant to have a meeting with Christa. Today's primary topic of discussion is my press kit. This is a compilation of material she sends to magazine editors and potential clients to generate both publicity and jobs. Her company logo is paired with mine on the outside of the folder, while inside we have a number of information sheets that provide

THIS ARTICLE IN ROLLING OUT WEEKLY MAGAZINE IS ABOUT ME AND MY COMPANY, STYLESBYMAXX.

important details on both of us. The introductory page has specific information on STYLESbyMAXX, while the biography page tells the reader who I am and how I got involved in this business. There's also a copy of a recent article that ran in a national entertainment newspaper, *Rolling Out Weekly*, plus a resume, photographic evidence of past work, and a business card from each of us. I love the design, which is hip, cute and eye-catching. This will prove to be another great marketing tool for my company, and all for only a $500 design fee.

Next up is a discussion of our plans to visit Los Angeles and New York City in a few months. We agree to research some mutually convenient dates and table our decision for a future meeting. We wrap things up by brainstorming additional marketing ideas, such as a new Web site separate from MySpace as well as redesigning our business cards.

THIS FOLDER WILL BE IN MY PRESS KIT. IT HAS MY COMPANY INFORMATION AND THAT OF MY PUBLICIST/BOOKING AGENT ON THE FRONT.

LESSONS/PROBLEMS

This turned out to be a very productive day, especially because Christa and I work so well together. Our vision about where we're going professionally is truly in synch. After explaining to me why I need a press kit and the importance of publicity, I understood how to increase my exposure to the people who are most likely to buy my services. More exposure in the right places means more jobs. It takes a lot of money to run a business, and I'm always careful with budgets to make sure that I have enough operating capital. One month I might have four jobs, while the next I might have only one or two. That means sticking to a budget is vital, but there's another old saying I believe in as well: "You only get out of something what you put into it."

PREDICTIONS

- *Work on my comp card*
- *Discuss business card revisions with Christa*
- *Check out several spring and summer fashion collections*

DIARY

I'll be working on two of my marketing tools today, a comp card and a new business card. My comp card is a promotional piece sent to clients when I want to generate leads. This will be the third one I've designed since starting my own business. I like to re-invent my card with every new group of jobs I do. The card sports color pictures of four or five of my best styling jobs, whether it's a photo shoot or a fashion consultation. In addition to picking out the best photos, I'll also need to decide on an attractive color scheme. Having collected flyers from several local suppliers of comp cards, one of my first decisions involves picking the best printing company. Prima printed the last one I designed. They did a wonderful job, but I always like to keep my options open. I'm working on a tight budget, so my best choice will be someone who can do the best job for the best price, and also offer me a fast turnaround. I want to have the finished cards in my hands no later than the middle of February. One hundred cards should be plenty, so I make some phone calls and get some price quotes.

I can't decide if I want a one-or two-sided card, and then there's the question of folding versus flat. Prices range from

MY 2006 COMP CARD.

between $100 to $225. I elect to stick with Prima since they're right in the ballpark and I trust their quality. My previous card was pink and brown, but I'll wait to select the color scheme after I decide which pictures to use. In addition to photos, the card will display my name and title, the name of my company, an e-mail address and MySpace link, plus Christa's contact information. The photos will set the tone for rest of the piece, and they'll also reflect the type of market I'm trying to develop. I enjoy having a diverse clientele, as I work with high-fashion photographers and all manner of musical artists from rock-and-roll to hip-hop. My photos need to grab the attention of each one of these client types while showing off my top wardrobe choices for each genre. After spending considerable time picking out my best five pictures, I elect to have one printed on the front of the card and four on the reverse. I can't quite make up my mind on colors, but that will keep for another day.

Now it's time to take a close look at my business card. It already looks great, so I don't want to make any drastic changes. I've decided to remove my toll-free phone number and add my booking agent's information. After a brief discussion with Christa on this topic, she tells me the graphic artist who's designing our press kit can also revise my business card. That's terrific news, since we'll probably qualify for a volume discount.

After spending three hours on revised marketing tools, I decide to look at the latest fashion trends. I've received a number of e-mails from designers, so I follow their embedded links to the Web sites that show off their newest items. My first visit is to see Gucci's 2007 spring and summer collection. They've done a beautiful job, with vibrant colors and patterns in the clothing items, and really cool shoes, sunglasses and handbags.

My next research leads me to a designer about which I know absolutely nothing. I'm always looking for something new and different, so Two Door Clothing draws my immediate attention. They prove to be a women's active-wear designer that is announcing a "Loco for Love" line, featuring the Speedy Gonzales cartoon character. Everything I see is fun and expressive, so when a client comes along for which this look would work, I'll definitely contact their public relations person.

LESSONS/PROBLEMS
My biggest problem today involved a decision for my comp

card's color scheme. It's better to sleep on it and make a wise decision rather than rushing into something I might regret later. These cards are one of my most important marketing tools, and everything has to look good and be right.

A LIST OF SUPPLIES I NEED FOR MY OFFICE.

Day 13 | *JANUARY 17*

PREDICTIONS

- *Update my stylist resume*
- *Contact Christa about updating my bio sheet*
- *Research designers*
- *Take inventory and decide what office supplies I need*

DIARY

My goal today is to update my resume. This is one of the most important documents in my portfolio. Even though many clients don't specifically ask to see a resume—they'll usually decide whether or not to use my services based on referrals or samples of my work—it's still a good document to have on hand. My resume has a much different look than the piece of paper one uses to get hired for a corporate-type position. It is basically a long list of all the people with whom I've worked in this industry. That includes the names of photographers who have shot my wardrobes, the recording artists and celebrities I've dressed, and all the other projects I've worked on. It's an eclectic group, encompassing music videos, print and television ads, promotions, movie premieres, television shows, and modeling agencies. At the top of my resume I post my contact information as well as Christa's. While I'm pleased with the way things look, it's obvious I need to hunt up more A-list clients. My bio still needs to be updated, but it's Christa's responsibility to write my bio so I ask her to work on it. She agrees to have it finished by the end of business tomorrow.

Researching designers is next on my list. I've received e-mail alerts for Gucci's fall and winter men's fashion show, plus Blance de Chine and Jimmy Choo. The Gucci collection looks great, and it occurs to me that many of their items will look good in a hip-hop setting. Their suits are very slick and classy in a vaguely European manner. Some of the suits even have fur accents on their collars, while the colors and fabrics they've used for the winter coats make them stand out from the rest of the collection.

After checking out Gucci, I move on to the Blanc de Chine site. I received an e-mail notice from Taryn, the company's marketing director, wanting to know if I had any upcoming projects that could use their clothing. The spring and summer collections feature a number of silk-screened dresses for women and lightweight jackets for men, and I'm offered an open invitation to pull whatever wardrobe I might need, whenever I need it. As a stylist, it's great to have a clothing company that's so excited about working with me. I check out the Web site and notice their new collection is significantly different from the other ones I've viewed over the past couple of days. It's based on traditional Chinese attire, a culture that's always intrigued me. Both the spring and summer collections feature soft fabrics with a shiny appearance, while still giving off that feeling of class. If any of my future projects offer an opportunity to use Chinese-inspired wardrobe items, I'll definitely go with Blanc de Chine.

The last designer I research is Jimmy Choo. I recently received an e-mail notice from Michelle, the Atlanta showroom rep. Most of their 2007 summer and spring items are already in stock, and they're also offering a fifty percent discount on autumn and winter shoes and handbags. One of the benefits of building these close relationships means hearing about sales before the public gets wind of them. I respond to both sales reps with thanks, telling them I'll be in touch whenever I have projects that would go well with their designer clothes or accessories.

For my final task of the day, I'll take office inventory and figure out what supplies I need. I end up putting a number of things on my shopping list. First there's carbon paper for my two-part forms, a cutting board on which to trim photos and tearsheets, updated resource books, and some file organizers and a new file cabinet. The most expensive items on my list are an all-in-one printer/fax/scanner, and a new laptop computer. This month's budget is tight, so I'll need to figure out what I need immediately and what can wait until next month. I decide the carbon paper is a must-have, as is the laptop. I'll start looking for a new computer next week, hoping I can get by with spending no more than $1100.

LESSONS/PROBLEMS

My limited budget prevented me from buying all the things I needed, once I did office inventory. Running a business is often a balancing act that makes you choose between what you need right now and what can wait until more revenue comes in the door.

Day 14 | JANUARY 18

PREDICTIONS
- *Work on my wardrobe contact book*
- *Do more online research*
- *Finalize my monthly office budget*

DIARY

It's another day to hang around the office, so I begin by organizing my wardrobe contact book. This book holds all the business cards I've collected from designer showrooms, boutiques and department stores, both from around town and across the country. I take a three-ring binder and place business card inserts into the notebook. I always visit the most popular malls and boutiques when I'm traveling, having heard about them from other people in the business or else seen their ads in various magazines. These business cards are a perfect reminder of who they are and where they're located. If I have a celebrity client in a specific city where I need to do some shopping, information like this is immediately accessible. Further, if a client of mine is seeking a high-end designer wardrobe or a store that's not located in Atlanta, I can use my wardrobe book to offer suggestions and options. I've also made room to post magazine articles or display ads from stores from which I haven't yet collected business cards. That list also includes designer showrooms and a roster of publicists who promote them. I organize my book into sections, titled high-end designers, jewelry, shoes, accessories, urban wear, men's fashions, and women's fashions. All my business cards are now organized and put

71

away where I can easily find them again. From this point forward, rather than letting them pile up I'll simply slide them into the proper spot in my wardrobe book for future reference.

All this organizational work takes me until three o'clock to accomplish, after which it's time to do some more online fashion research. I decide to check out the Lebook Web site, which has collected all the latest ad campaigns and includes links to the agencies that represent them as well as the names of the creative team that worked on their campaigns. This proves to be a great research tool, since it has all this important information in one easy-to-access location. I'm registered to receive their monthly newsletter, which alerts me via e-mail whenever they happen to post a new ad campaign. I see several interesting ads on the Lebook site and mark down the names of the responsible ad agencies for Christa. She'll follow up with them and see if they're interested in creating a business relationship with us.

I close out the day by working on my office budget. First I make note of my recurring monthly expenses such as utilities, Internet access, cell phone, and office supplies. Office supplies are one of my biggest expenses, and I calculate I'll need more than $1800 to beef up my inventory. The rest of the items on that list run me about $245 a month. Next I add up more specialized costs, including travel and marketing items. From a marketing standpoint I need comp cards and envelopes, photo reprints, portfolios, postage, new press kits, and Web site expenditures.

WHERE TO WEAR IS A GREAT SHOPPING GUIDE OF STORES AND BOUTIQUES IN DIFFERENT CITIES.

Marketing will easily run me $2500. Travel costs are next. Christa and I will need hotel rooms, rental cars and an entertainment allowance when we fly to Los Angeles and New York City to do our networking. Also, I need a passport because my TV job will take me out of the country. My estimate for travel expenses is $2200. Over the next four months I'll need to spend $7480 on running my business. That works out to $1870 a month, which is a more manageable way of looking at things. And if a big project comes up during that time which pays me a lot of money, I'll be able to accelerate my spending and pick up the more expensive items I need sooner.

LESSONS/PROBLEMS

It sure is expensive to run a business. Having a realistic budget gives me a true sense of what I need and where my money goes every month. It's important that I make sensible business and personal choices when it comes to

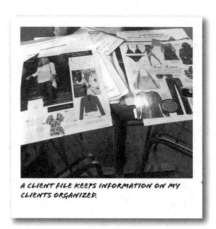

A CLIENT FILE KEEPS INFORMATION ON MY
CLIENTS ORGANIZED.

spending my hard-earned cash. I've found that the best
way to plan ahead involves building a quarterly budget and
dividing up costs over that four-month period, even though
I'd love to buy everything I need at one time.

PREDICTIONS

- *Do online research to seek out various spring and summer collections*
- *Work on my passport application*

DIARY

This is a day set aside for research, as I have a number of designer collections to check out. Fashion stylists have to be up on what's hot and what's not, and I need to be able to identify the "in" designers and know how to put my hands on their material. At the Trafik trade show a few months ago, I spoke to the rep from Seamless Showroom. Recently I received an e-mail notice of their line called Fighting Eel, which prompts me to check out their Web site. I'm delighted to discover they carry nine lines including this one. It's always more convenient when multiple collections are visible on a single site. Other posted data includes press kits, line sheets, and what days of the week their fashion items are available for viewing. Fighting Eel features a variety of sexy dresses in vibrant colors. Styles include strapless, halter-top and spaghetti-strap. They even have jumpers.

Another Seamless Showroom line is Michelle Jonas, with outfits that offer a fairly Bohemian feel. Peasant-style clothes are definitely where it's at for Michelle Jonas, with earth-tone-colored skirts and dresses in lightweight material such as linen. Then there is Lauren Jane, which offers dresses that are formal as well as others that are more casual. Some of

INSTYLE: SECRETS OF STYLE, ELEMENTS OF
STYLE BY CELEBRITY STYLIST PHILLIP BLOCH
AND SOUL STYLE ARE AMONG THE FASHION
BOOKS THAT TEACH, INSPIRE AND MOTIVATE ME.

these would be great for less-intensive red-carpet events,
such as the MTV awards or the Grammys. The Lauren Jane
press release mentions two of the celebrities who've worn
their dresses—Nikki Hilton and Eva Mendes. The dress Nikki
Hilton wore only cost $258. The Alisha Levine collection
has tops and necklaces. This line doesn't especially interest
me, so I decide to move on to Bilingual. They're showing
a variety of prints inspired by Spanish, Hawaiian and Asian
accents, thus the name. I could see an eclectic artist like
Kelis or someone exotic-looking such as Eva Langoria
wearing a piece from this collection. I will definitely move
Seamless Showroom to the top of my wardrobe contact list.

My next online stop is the *Style* Web site. Here it's possible
to link to fashion show sites, check out different designers
and their collections, uncover new fashion trends, and read
about fashion as it relates to the world of entertainment.
This week's newsletter offers a neat feature, the opportunity

to create a personalized "look" book. I can collect pictures of my top design picks from the *Style* site and post them on a personal page for the whole world to see. That's incredibly cool! I don't have time today to do it, but I'll definitely put one together in a day or two.

One of the online articles discusses the outfits seen on the red carpet at the recent Golden Globe Awards, making note of which celebrity wore which designer's creation. Vera Wang and Alexander McQueen were just two of the designers featured there. An article like this is an excellent resource for me, especially if I missed seeing the event on television. Each designer is mentioned by name, which means I don't have to guess or continually run back and forth on my TiVO. The accessories section of the newsletter discusses the new shoe trend that emphasizes patent leather uppers and metallic heels. One illustrated example is a Bill Blass mogul shoe with a gold heel. The overall design doesn't do much for me, but I'll consider the metallic heel a must-have the next time I'm shopping for shoes. My favorite part of the *Style* newsletter is their quarterly trend report. The Spring 2007 issue not only reveals the latest trends for this spring, but it also has tons of photos from the runway show where they spotted these trends in the first place. The newsletter identifies romantic silk fabrics and futuristic metallics as the hot spring materials, plus wardrobes inspired by the 1940s and 1980s.

Because of my job with *Get Married* TV, I'll be traveling internationally. It's about time I owned a passport anyway, since being part of the entertainment field may require me

THIS IS THE APPLICATION AND LIST OF DOCUMENTS I NEED TO GET MY PASSPORT TO TRAVEL ABROAD.

to work abroad more often. I should be prepared to fly off at a moment's notice, and I need a passport to do that. The application I picked up at my post office is confusing, so I visit the Web site to better understand the requirements and costs. I learn it can take from three to eight weeks to obtain a passport from a local post office, but that time can be trimmed to two weeks if I apply in person at a regional passport agency. The closest one to me is in New Orleans, which is 500 miles away. I could pay for expedited service, which guarantees a three-week time frame. But that will add considerably to the cost, especially when you factor in the price of two passport photos and overnight delivery. Here's the bottom line. I can spend $112.00 and get my passport in six to eight weeks, or spend $200.80 and receive it in two to three weeks. Fortunately I have all the documents I need in my immediate possession, including a certified copy of my birth certificate. I have the phone number of a place that takes passport photos, and I leave a callback number with them so I can find out how much they'll cost.

LESSONS/PROBLEMS

I discovered some really hot designer collections online today, while also exploring fashion trends for the upcoming spring season. Online research is one of my most valuable stylist tools. Because I'm taping my TV show soon, I need a passport quickly. I was disappointed to discover how long the process takes, and I'll have to pay extra to get it expedited within a three-week period. However, traveling to New Orleans to speed up the process is not a cost-effective option.

PREDICTIONS

- *Make contact with people at the Get Married TV show*
- *Collect corporate tax information*
- *Update my portfolio*

DIARY

Dionne is responsible for looking after the combined wardrobe, makeup and hair department at the *Get Married* TV show, where I've been hired to do the fashion styling. She calls to tell me the start of the shooting schedule has been pushed back to the middle of February, a four-week delay. The show's producer has already started to put the elements together to get things moving, and I'm reminded I'll need a passport since we're filming several of the episodes outside the United States. Dionne is glad to hear I've already begun the process. We discuss how payroll will be distributed—on a direct-deposit basis—and she offers to send over the forms so I can get signed up. We've worked together on other projects, and I'm excited about the chance to continue our business relationship.

I also hear from the show's production assistant. They've received my wardrobe agreement and she compliments me on its professional appearance. However, the producer has some suggestions as to how we can streamline the wardrobe process, including the addition of login sheets. We also discuss various shoe options for the hosts. I'm working on signing up a shoe sponsor, which means we'd get foot attire

HIGH FASHION PHOTOS FROM MY PORTFOLIO.

for free or at a serious discount. She's happy to hear that. We both agree that four pairs should do it; pumps in black and brown, plus sandals in those two colors as well.

With my tax deadline approaching, it's time to get my paperwork in order. First I pull out my tax file, which contains my receipt envelopes as well as copies of past returns. Now that I'm a sole proprietor, I'm still learning this whole tax-payment game. It's soon apparent that I've done a poor job of sorting my receipts throughout the past fiscal year. Even though everything is in the proper month's file, nothing much is organized by the type of expense. Different categories receive different tax treatments in the eyes of the I.R.S., so sorting receipts by type is necessary. I make separate piles for meal expenses, travel, office costs, rent, telephone, and entertainment. After meeting with an accountant, I'll have a better idea of which expenses are deductible and at what rate. The next items on my list are the sheets for payables and receivables. These get matched to my bank statements, which allows me to tie together expenditures with a particular check or payment. I'm pretty good at holding on to all this material, but organizing it properly is another thing. The final bits of paperwork to place into the box are all the 1099 forms I received from clients. I've heard that companies don't issue these declarations unless you've done more than $600 worth of work for them, but I'll let the accountant answer all my questions. A friend of mine, like me a small-business owner, referred me to the accountant who did her business taxes last year. I'll call in a few days to make an appointment.

My portfolio needs some extensive updating, even though it's come a long way since I started in this business. This is the book I use to validate my work. It describes who I am, creatively, as a fashion stylist. I need to include more commercial work, perhaps an ad campaign or some catalogue material. I've posted tearsheets on my hip-hop clientele, some high-fashion photos, and several edgy yet glamorous lingerie shots. I see I'm missing the photos we shot for the CD cover of GRITS, a hip-hop group, so I vow to e-mail the art director for copies. This is my first major recording group, so I'm proud to show off the CD cover.

A number of factors go into the production of a good portfolio. I'm putting together three complete sets—one "original" and two spares. For the cover I use leather-bound 9 x 12 folders. Pictures in the main book will be printed on professional-quality photo paper, although I can get by

MY TAX FILES HOLD IMPORTANT DOCUMENTS AND RECEIPTS. THEY KEEP ME ORGANIZED AND PREPARED FOR TAX SEASON.

with laser prints for the spare copies. There's no reason to spend $10 to $15 for top-notch photos in my backup books, in case they get lost or damaged. Decent laser prints can be had for as little as a dollar apiece. With around twenty images per book, that extra cost can add up fast. Unfortunately, the company I've been using for several years to print my photos is shutting down. There's no point in giving them additional business if they won't be around to serve me in the future. One more item on my to-do list—find a new photo-printing vendor.

LESSONS/PROBLEMS

Today was quite productive for me. I got my tax information organized and I worked on my portfolio. As a business owner, keeping track of taxes is a lot more challenging than if I worked in a salaried position. Once I get together with an accountant, I'll have a greater understanding of the process and should do a better job of keeping track of my expenses for next year. Because it's important to have high-quality photo prints, I'll be extra-careful about choosing a printing company to replace the one that's going out of business. If the color isn't perfect, the perception people have of the work I do will suffer. I'll check with my photographer friends for some referrals.

PREDICTIONS

- *Update and organize my paperwork files*
- *Read magazines for research*
- *Check out spring fashions at the mall*
- *Catch up on music videos and entertainment shows*

DIARY

The electronic versions of my business documents need updating, and I should also figure out a way to save them in one convenient place. I start by creating a STYLESbyMAXX master folder. I'll need two separate versions of a confirmation agreement—one for clients who rent wardrobe items, and another for those who buy them. My artist information sheet and my client sheet both look good, so they will remain unchanged. I've stored paperwork files everywhere—on various disks plus on my desktop. This makes no sense, so I collect everything and save it to a single storage device. Now my confirmation agreements, client and artist information sheets, employment forms, stylist letters, fax cover sheets, letterhead templates and tearsheet collection forms are all on a single disk. If I don't have my laptop with me, carrying around this disk means I'll be able to run into a copy store and pull up everything I need.

Doing magazine research is one of my favorite tasks. Who are the hottest photographers right now? Which stylists are dressing which A-list artists and entertainers? What are next season's fashion trends? These questions are answered

SOME OF THE MOST IMPORTANT THINGS IN MY OFFICE ARE ON MY DESK.

A SHEET WITH THE ARTIST'S MUSIC INFORMATION AND PROJECT INFORMATION.

in the various publications I read every month, including a couple of hip-hop magazines and three or four basic fashion journals. I might spend as much as $50 a month to feed my habit, buying them at newsstands or grocery stores around Atlanta. Today's research takes me to *Elle* and *GQ* for fashion and *XXL* and *Vibe Vixen* for hip-hop culture. *Elle* usually has the best fashion spreads, while *GQ* is clearly the top men's fashion journal in the business. Many people consider *Vogue* to be the fashion industry's bible, especially since

HIP HOP CULTURE MAGAZINES PROVIDE GREAT IDEAS FOR PROJECTS.

all the major designers advertise there. The articles they run are equally informative. *Lucky* is a personal shopper's dream reference guide. Each magazine has something unique to offer, which is why I check out so many different ones each month. The latest issue of *GQ* is showing off the newest spring basics, highlighting hooded sweatshirts, leather bomber jackets, white-on-white sneakers, and some stylishly cut business suits. This month's *Elle* is a monster magazine, with 530 pages of must-have springtime women's fashions. They're showing me that fringed trim-and-tassel accessories from the 1970s are making a comeback, as are white handbags. *Vibe Vixen* is geared toward women's hip-hop fashions, and their current issue features bracelets made of bronze and gold as well as a number of bright red accessories. Meanwhile, *XXL* does the same thing for male hip-hoppers, emphasizing the hottest sneaker designs and men's urban wear. Because I do so much business in the hip-hop realm, both of these magazines help me a lot when it comes to styling my artist clients.

Looking at pictures in magazines is one thing, but the best way to judge fashion is by seeing the clothes in person. It's time to hit the malls and lay my hands on some actual outfits and accessories. Phipps Plaza is an upscale mall, one of my favorite places to find high-end designer wardrobe items. My first stop there is at NikeTown. They stock all the classic sneaker models, such as Air Jordan, Air Force One and Air Max. Jimmy Choo also has a store at Phipps, but Michelle, the showroom rep, has the day off. The gold shoe collection I saw online looks even better in person, and a matching gold purse is spectacular. This item will have to wait for a serious A-list client, since only the fairly wealthy would be willing to spend $7000 for a purse.

Juicy Couture, a shop best known for terrycloth handbags and jogging suits, is next. The sales associate shows me some cute spring items, but more are on the way and should be on display in a couple of weeks. Both the Gucci and the Elie Tahari stores are showing spring collections rich in brown, red and beige. Handbags and sunglasses are my favorite items at Gucci, and I like the blazers and jackets by Elie Tahari. This mall had a lot of women's items worth seeing, but nothing for men. I hope I'll have better luck at my next stop.

Lenox Square is the most popular mall in Atlanta. They boast high-end stores such as Neiman Marcus and Louis Vuitton, plus mid-range department stores like Bloomingdale and Macy's. There are also a number of smaller franchise

FASHION MAGAZINES ARE MY INSPIRATION!

I LOVE THE UPSCALE AND HIGH-END DEPARTMENT
STORES IN PHIPPS PLAZA.

stores like Ralph Lauren, Bakers (for shoes) and BeBe, but
none of these has much in the way of spring fashions yet.
The visit to Lenox is not a total loss, because I introduce
myself to one of the sales associates at David Yurman, a
jewelry store, who might be a worthwhile contact for future
photo shoots.

After coming home I decide to catch up with some videos
on MTV. Watching videos is fun as well as educational,

since it gives me a good look at current fashion trends in the music business. I find additional TV research sources on the E! Network's various entertainment shows, especially those that broadcast red-carpet footage.

LESSONS/PROBLEMS

I would have saved time today by waiting for notification from showroom reps and sales associates regarding the availability of new spring fashions. Since many of the items hadn't yet been put on display, I felt I wasted my time by go to the mall without first doing my homework.

PREDICTIONS
- *Update my trend board*
- *Meet with Lakeisha to revise her resume and her portfolio*

DIARY

Today I plan to work on my trend board, something I keep in my office to post photos of the latest fashion trends. This helps remind me what's hot so I can incorporate these looks in current and upcoming projects. My first task is to go back through the magazines I looked at over the past couple of days, tearing out previously marked pages that have the sort of outfits I find worth consideration. These pages contain a variety of items, with an emphasis on women's accessories and trousers, plus men's business suits.

While checking e-mail I notice a message from my friend, DJ Irie. He has designed a limited-edition sneaker for Adidas that will likely be considered a collector's item. I store this information in my DJ Irie X file in case, I have a client who might wish to purchase a pair or if a project comes along where these shoes might match the rest of the wardrobe I've assembled. Then it's time to call my assistant, Lakeisha, to confirm our meeting today. She agrees to stop by around six o'clock so we can look over her resume and revise her portfolio.

Lakeisha is interested in submitting her resume to a magazine, and she wants my professional opinion before

MY TREND BOARD HAS TEAR SHEETS OF POPULAR STYLES OF THE SEASON POSTED ON IT.

sending it to them. After considerable discussion regarding what she hopes to accomplish, we agree her resume looks great and needs no revision. Next we look at a number of images she styled during a recent test shoot. This involved a male model employed by the local branch of a national agency, and Lakeisha designed three separate looks for the session. She wants my help in selecting the best possible photos to include in her professional portfolio. We spend quite a bit of time examining each picture in great detail. My advice is to use only two of the looks, since those show off her skills the best, and we narrow down the number of pictures to just a couple for each look.

LESSONS/PROBLEMS

Today was one of those short workdays that remind me why it's such a pleasure to run my own business. There were no problems for me to solve, and I didn't have to worry about deadlines or difficult clients. Updating my trend board will definitely help me keep track of the hottest seasonal trends for any upcoming projects.

PREDICTIONS
- *Weekly conference call with Christa*
- *Take delivery on the Insights Marketing swimsuit designs*
- *Create a look book on the Style Web site*

DIARY

My primary goal today involves wrapping up the swimsuit project I'm doing for Insights Marketing, but first I have my weekly telephone discussion with Christa, my booking agent. Our initial focus is on the *Get Married* TV program. We're both pleased they've committed to thirteen episodes, which is the sort of regular work every fashion stylist loves to have. The program airs on Women's Entertainment Television beginning the first of April, broadcast every Sunday at 9:30 A.M. Eastern Time. I'm still waiting to receive the shooting schedule from Dionne, and I promise to send it along to Christa as soon as it's in my hands. Our conference call is short today because I need to get ready for my meeting with Mychael Knight, the fashion designer. He wants me to see the swimsuits he's put together for the liquor promotion. Keshia Walker, who runs Insights, told me by e-mail she'll have to miss our meeting but will send her assistant instead.

We meet at the Insights Marketing office, where Mychael has arrived ahead of me and is already setting out the swimsuits, separated by color. Everything looks terrific, and Keshia's assistant agrees with my assessment. I trade real-time e-mails with Keshia, where I tell her the swimsuits are on hand and perfectly suit her client's needs, while she responds with her thanks to both of us for meeting the deadline and doing such a good job of matching the client's color choices.

Back at my home office, I follow up on the opportunity presented by the *Style* Web site and build my own look book. I create a user account and then review the various designer collections posted on the site. My personalized book shows off the new fashion trend toward metallic colors, and I select different items by such design houses as Gucci, John Galliano, Marc Jacobs, and Prada. Anyone can now visit this site, view all the look books created by various stylists, and vote for their favorites. I hope people enjoy seeing my fun and creative material.

Then it's time to catch up on fashion news. I receive a regular e-newsletter from the *Fashion Week Daily* Web site, which reports on all kinds of news and events that are taking place in the worldwide fashion industry. For example, I read that one of my favorite design teams, Dean and Dan Caten of D-Squared, have decided to open a flagship store in Milan. It will occupy a 5,382-square-foot store in the heart of Italy's most exciting fashion city, where they plan to emphasize accessories and ready-to-wear clothing. Another article mentions that *Teen Vogue* magazine has hired a new fashion editor. This is good to know, since now I have the name of the person over there to receive my comp card. It's always better to forward marketing materials to a specific person rather than simply addressing it to "Fashion Editor."

Another bit of news involves Karl Lagerfeld, who is doing some design work for Fendi and will have two runway shows to display his collection. One show would not have accommodated the number of people they expect to attend this exciting preview.

LESSONS/PROBLEMS

I was glad to wrap up the Insights swimwear project, with the suits deemed acceptable and turned over to the marketing company ahead of schedule. Keeping a regular eye on what's happening in the fashion world does a great service to my clients, who want to make sure they're wearing only the latest and hottest wardrobe items.

PREDICTIONS

- *Organize my office files*
- *Check and reply to e-mails*
- *Assist a personal-shopper client*

DIARY

My first task this morning is to put away all the items that have been piling up in my file box. Staying organized is a key strategy for me, but one I don't always follow as faithfully as I should. These files are sorted into separate piles according to type—project name, marketing information, photographer, personal details, or expenses. Reaching the bottom of the file tray is a victory for me, because it means I'll know where to find something the next time I need to look for it.

In the midst of my organizing I received a call from Keja, one of my clients who is a well-known host and model. She plans to attend a swanky party in New York City and needs help in finding just the right dress and accessories. She has a second dress already picked out, but needs advice on which boots would look best with it. We arrange a meeting for later this afternoon.

Looking over my e-mail inbox, I see a message from a person who represents Conspiracy Eight, a clothing line. My name and e-mail address are contained in dozens of databases, which makes it easy for me to keep up with the latest fashion trends. The rep notifies me that the company's spring and summer collection is now posted on their Web site. How did we ever manage to stay informed before the Internet? I quickly visit the site and check out the collection, which is a beautiful assemblage of silk clothes.

Keja and I meet at three o'clock to discuss her wardrobe needs. First I need to know more about the event she's attending. She repeats what she said on the phone, which is that it's a swanky party in New York that will require her to look classy, sexy and drop-dead gorgeous. I pull out several magazines I'd brought along for reference, and we go through them together to get some ideas. For her part, she pulls out some tearsheets that depict styles she admires. I make a note of her dress and shoe size, and we also discuss deadlines. She'll need to have these items in her possession no later than February 7. I'm also reminded that she needs an additional pair of boots to go with a second dress, and I make note of the outfit's description so I'll know what to look for. I promise I'll get back to her with some firm ideas in the next couple of days, making sure she knows everything will get done well ahead of her deadline.

LESSONS/PROBLEMS

As soon as I wrap up a project, it's important that I file the client folder immediately. It takes way more time to put away a whole stack of folders that have accumulated over time than it does to stick one in its proper place as soon as I'm finished with it. Organization is the key!

PREDICTIONS

- *Work on the Get Married folder*
- *Send personal details to the Style Network*
- *Research fashion Web sites*

DIARY

Since the *Get Married* TV show will begin taping soon,
I decide it's time to assemble the client folder. The first
material I insert is a list of the production team members.
I'm the wardrobe stylist and Lakeisha is my assistant, plus
there are two makeup artists and a hairstylist. The head of
the department is Dionne. The two show hosts are Jessica
and Jenn. The show has its own Web site, so I check it out
to familiarize myself with the image they've created, along
with the planned storyline. The network that's airing the
show, Women's Entertainment Television, is also a factor in
the sort of wardrobe decisions I'll wish to make, so I visit that
site as well. I'm interested to see that the clothing designs
I choose for the hosts will match the type of people who
tune into this network. You don't want the attire worn on
a show's set to clash with the image the network executives
have imagined. I print out all the appropriate Web site
pages and place them into the folder, which means I'll be
able to refer to them without logging onto the Internet
every time.

Then I go through the magazines Jessica and Jenn looked
through when we did our first consultation. At the time

I matched the tearsheets that each woman selected to their individual client sheets. Each of them has an entirely different taste in clothing, and I'm careful not to mix the styles. Jenn prefers a more conservative look, while Jessica likes to wear flashier outfits. It will be a challenge to satisfy their individual interests without having them clash on camera. The last items I insert in the folder are the e-mails I received from Dionne in reference to our wardrobe discussions. As more material comes in, I'll be sure to add that as well.

After logging onto my e-mail server, I see that Christa had forwarded a message from the Style Network. They're casting for an Atlanta-based television show to be called *Style School,* and they're seeking women between the ages of 18 and 40 with a good sense of fashion and style who also love to go shopping. The program will share this information with viewers in several different ways. They want women to display and share their views on fashion and beauty. There is no actual school involved; the title refers to the fact that the women they select they will "school" the TV audience on their fashion views. This is an exciting opportunity for me. I love to shop, I know style, and I have strong views about fashion. I send over all the information they request, which includes my contact details, several photos, and a short essay about why I want to do this show. I'm looking forward to hearing back from them. The Style Network is one of my favorite channels and I've always wanted to be featured on one of their shows. Maybe this is the chance for me?

Finally, I read over the newsletter I receive regularly from the *Style* Web site. This issue happens to feature a comprehensive preview of the New York Fall 2007 Fashion Week. The information on this Web site is incredibly helpful, and it's updated regularly. Thanks to my careful reading today, I learn that designer Marc Jacobs will show his new collection only in London this year, rather than anywhere in the States. The preview also shows me which models will be the new faces on the runway this fall, what new-style handbag will be hot, and which designers will donate their proceeds to a charity that's a major focus for Fall 2007 Fashion Week.

LESSONS/PROBLEMS

The fashion world is miles ahead of the regular world when it comes to the calendar. Even though it's only January, there are plenty of details out there on next fall's top designs. I've found the *Style* Web site to be a great place to see all the important faces, places and artwork that inspire the most influential designers and their collections.

Day 22 | JANUARY 29

PREDICTIONS
- Check with a former client for portfolio items
- Meet with my personal shopper client

DIARY

My first task today is to reach out to Eddy at Boerhaus Creative for copies of the GRITS CD I need for my portfolio. While reviewing my tearsheet collection I noticed I was missing the series of pictures that catalogued the GRITS photo shoot we did for their CD cover. I was the person responsible for styling that shoot. He apologizes for the oversight and promises to send these CDs to me as soon as possible. This is my first official CD cover, and I'm excited about adding it to my collection.

I've already caught up on reviewing my fashion newsletters as well as a bunch of MySpace messages. After checking my e-mail account and responding to a couple of inquiries, it's time to prepare for my appointment with Keja. I pull out the notes I made when we spoke earlier about her need for a party dress. We meet at one o'clock, and I begin by laying out several of the ideas I brainstormed after our conversation the other day. We discuss which colors would look best on her, based on skin tone and other factors, and I also suggest she might want to wear her hair "up." Also, open-toed shoes are really big this season, which she didn't know, and the weather in New York is likely to be stormy so she should count on bringing along a nice trench coat. She agrees to each one of my suggestions, and I advise her that I'll have everything assembled well ahead of her deadline.

After we part I drive over to Lenox Square Mall to see what's in the stores, especially dresses. After more than an hour of wandering from one boutique to another, I make note of a few things that would look decent on Keja, but not spectacular. I'll have to try some of my other favorite spots. While at the mall I decide to visit the Apple store. I'm in the market for a new laptop, and the Mac Book seems to be my best bet. I spot a white 13'-inch version for $1099, which is just about the amount I have in my budget for a computer. I'm glad when things like that work out in my favor.

LESSONS/PROBLEMS

Today was a fairly easy one, with no major problems to solve. Even though I didn't find the right dress for Keja, we still have plenty of time for that and a lot more stores to check before I get worried. I'm confident I'll have her looking fabulous in plenty of time for her New York party.

PREDICTIONS

- *Meet again with my personal shopping client*
- *Watch a movie for fashion research*

DIARY

Keja and I agree to meet at Lenox Square Mall in mid-afternoon. In this morning's newspaper I read that Macy's is having a sale on women's boots, and we need something stylish for her New York trip to match the dress she owns. After checking e-mail and MySpace, I pull out Keja's folder so I can take it with me on our shopping excursion. Having my notes with me will make our search a bit easier.

At three o'clock I meet Keja in the shoe department at Macy's. After taking a close look at the dress she's brought, I decide she'll also need a belt to help define her waist as well as fishnet stockings to cover the space between the tops of her boots and the hem of the dress. We spend a lot of effort looking around the department and trying on several pairs of boots. Because the dress is black, I suggest she'll need a boot that will provide interesting contrast without clashing with it. Macy's has a metallic gray boot with a red heel, and I can see a red belt going perfectly with this outfit. The salesman disappears for a few minutes, only to report back that he doesn't have Keja's size in stock. After calling around to other Macy's stores in the metro area, he finds a pair in the correct size at Arbor Place Mall, a 30-minute drive away. After a brief consultation, we decide it's

MY PERSONAL SHOPPING CLIENT, KEJA IN THE SHOE DEPARTMENT AT MACY'S. LOOKING FOR THE RIGHT BOOTS IS OUR MISSION TODAY!

worth the trip because these boots are perfect for her. But before departing we check out several mall stores for just the right belt. Keja tries on a few, but nothing speaks to us. I mention I'll do some more looking around this week.

Having Keja with me while I'm shopping is an exception to my general rule. I usually take my clients along with me because I feel it interferes with the creative process, and I'd rather do that on my own. My standard procedure is to pick things up, meet the client for a fitting session away from the store, and then return whatever doesn't fit or might not look its best. Today's session worked out well, however, because Keja let me be the stylist and work creatively. She stood aside until I invited her over to try something on, rather than running around the store asking, "What about this?" or, "Do you like that?" That's irritating, but today Keja was the perfect client.

Since it's a fair drive to the other store, we decide to ride together. The salesman is waiting for us, and the boots are already out on the counter. Keja tries them on after changing into her dress, and everything looks terrific. On our way back to Lenox to pick up my car, I remind her I'll hunt down a red belt and the fishnet stockings before she leaves for New York City next week.

Later I decide to go see *Dreamgirls*. As soon as I heard they were making the movie I knew I had to see it. Not only does it tell an exciting story with great music, but I'm anxious to see the fashions designed for the cast. I enjoy doing this type of research because movies always inspire my style, my creative thought process, and my personal life. The film is set in the 1960s, and I find the costumes offer a perfect look at that era. Each of the main characters has a different style, and the designers do a great job matching their outfits with their personalities.

LESSONS/PROBLEMS

Even though Macy's didn't have the boots Keja wanted, the clerk was extremely helpful by finding her size in a different store across town. The drive was well worth the effort, because now she has the perfect boots to go with the perfect dress.

Day 24 | *JANUARY 31*

PREDICTIONS
- *Organize my e-mail inboxes*
- *Shop for my personal shopping client*

DIARY

I'm up early this morning so I can sort through my e-mail before spending the rest of the day shopping for Keja's dress. Like most people, I own multiple e-mail accounts— some are personal, while others are work-related. After logging on I decide that some of these messages should be saved for future reference, while the rest can be trashed. The best way to organize this is to create separate folders for each topic and then stick those e-mails into each labeled folder. I make individual folders for my booking agent and my assistant, plus dividers for client contracts, designer showrooms, fashion press information, personal shopping clients, fashion styling clients, and travel links. From this point forward, whenever I have an e-mail that needs to be saved, I'll stick it into the appropriate folder rather than scroll through the whole list to find it.

I contact Keja to let her know I'm headed out today to find her a dress. We agree on February 2 as a fitting date, which means I need to find something for her a.s.a.p. My first stop is Cumberland Mall, which has some stores that aren't found anywhere else in the Atlanta area. Looking through the racks of dresses, I come across one that has the right mix of colors and soft fabric that should look great with

Keja's complexion. It's classy, with just the right amount of sex appeal. Naturally I'll need Keja to come in and try on the dress, but we can worry about that later. Before leaving the store I ask the sales clerk to set it aside, and tell her I'll check with my client later to arrange a fitting. I'm in the market for some cute accessories to go with this dress, so I cruise several other stores in the mall to pick up some ideas. However, I won't actually buy anything until Keja agrees to buy this dress.

During my wandering I receive a follow-up e-mail on my PDA from the publicist putting on a children's fashion show that will feature up to a hundred young models. I see they're trying to firm up a date and venue, after which they'll let me know if I'm to be hired as the show's stylist. I'm glad to have heard back from her, as it's been several weeks since we last discussed this project. I know there are times when a project is held up because additional information is required before the organizers can give it the green light. I wasn't worried, however, because there always seems to be another project for me around the next corner. If it's meant to be, I figure I'll get the job. Some I win and some I lose. When I first started out in this business, I heard "no" a lot more times than "yes." But now that I have more experience, I've found people are more willing to take a chance on hiring a new fashion stylist.

I leave around four o'clock for the ten-mile drive to Perimeter Mall. Even though I think I've found what may be the perfect dress, I prefer to have multiple options whenever I'm deciding on a wardrobe. And though there are some nice dresses at this mall, nothing looks as good as the one I had set aside at Cumberland. I'm so convinced this is the one, I call Keja immediately and describe it for her in great detail over the phone. Based upon my description, she's equally excited to see it. We'll meet at the store on February 2, and I'll try to have shoes and accessories picked out at the same time so she can see what everything looks like together.

LESSONS/PROBLEMS

Even though I found the perfect dress at the first place I visited today, it was still better to explore other options. Most of the time I have a feeling when I see something and know it's going to work, and it certainly is time-consuming to run from one mall to another. But my personal-shopper clients are paying me to do just that, so it's only right that they get this superior level of service. And besides, I might see something today I'll remember for another client down the road.

PREDICTIONS

- *Create New Year objectives*
- *Work on business goals*

DIARY

I've decided to set today aside as the perfect time to establish objectives for the rest of the year, a very important task for my company and me. If I don't make a point of planning for my future, I'll be unable to concentrate on the things I need to accomplish. Then there are days when I'm frustrated with my career, and getting through them is easier when I have a positive focus. My main objective for 2007 is to expand my clientele in the fashion and entertainment industry. I want to sign up A-list clients, which could include top musical artists or Hollywood actors. These people have much bigger budgets to work with, and my association with them would give my company greater exposure. Another objective involves branding my company. Whenever someone thinks of fashion or a fashion stylist, I want STYLESbyMAXX or the name Kim Maxwell to come immediately to mind.

Setting goals is next. When I first set out to pursue my dream as a fashion stylist, I had no sense of direction. Even though I knew what sort of clientele I wanted to attract, I never took the time to analyze what it would take to get me there. It was a process of trial-and-error all along the way. Had I given my career more thought at the beginning, I'm sure I'd be even more successful today. I begin this exercise by writing down my personal goals for this year, which is dominated by my intention to earn more money. I've created a company budget, so I know how much it will take to get my office in order. A smarter marketing campaign, a more attractive comp card and better publicity will all add up to more opportunities. The more work I generate, the more money I earn—it's that simple.

A balanced existence is also important, so I decide my career should occupy sixty percent of my life, while my family and friends will take up the remainder. The split stands at fifty-fifty today. Even though everyone in my life gives me lots of support, my career is what truly makes me happy. At this point I feel I'm giving my company about a ninety percent effort, which is simply not acceptable. I must strive to hit that hundred percent mark to achieve my final goal, which involves taking my career to the next level. This level involves signing up A-list clients, being in demand for more high profile jobs, and showing more creativity.

My career goals for 2007 are more specific. I want at least three celebrity clients, to see my material published in at least four magazines—one local and three national—to style three ad campaigns, and to be featured on television as a fashion stylist. I believe these are all attainable, since I'm much more experienced and have started to make a name for myself in the industry. I plan to discuss these goals with my booking agent, Christa. She'll act as my support system as well as be the person who helps me reach this new level of success. With Christa aware of my goals, she'll also understand in which direction to take my bookings.

Toward the end of the day I call Christa and read to her what I've written. She believes these goals are very realistic, commenting further that some have been set into motion by us staying in touch with the West Coast-based actor. He would be a terrific celebrity client for me, plus there's the work I'm doing on *Get Married* TV as the key fashion stylist. After our conversation I feel both inspired and optimistic. It's great to know that my booking agent understands my vision and is willing to do whatever it takes to help me reach my goals. Later I type up my thoughts and post them on my work board, where I'll see the list every day. By having these plans right in front of me, I'll be constantly reinforced.

LESSONS/PROBLEMS
Writing down goals can be very therapeutic, and it also serves to put me back on the right track. I love the fact that my booking agent is solidly behind me and is willing to accept my goals as her own. Sometimes all I need is a little motivation to keep me going.

PREDICTIONS

- *Research fashion trends*
- *Meet with my client for a dress fitting*
- *Attend a fashion and entertainment industry event*

DIARY

At three o'clock Keja and I plan to get together at Cumberland Mall for her dress fitting. Before that, however, I have time to devote to researching current fashion trends. There are plenty of Web sites to check out, and I always enjoy reading different media resources to learn what's going on in the fashion world. I see that today is National "Wear Red" Day, which is designed to raise awareness of heart disease in women. Since it's Mercedes Benz Fashion Week in New York City, the car manufacturer is sponsoring a fashion show in Bryant Park where designers will feature red dresses. This is news to me, but I appreciate the concept behind it all. Fashion can be far more than who is the top designer and what are the hot items right now. The industry has found a way to bring women's health issues to the forefront, such as breast cancer and now heart disease. I've attended Fashion Week in past years, and I'm sad to have missed out in 2007. It's exciting to see all the new designs firsthand, meet the designers in person, and attend all the events sponsored by the industry's major fashion houses.

The *Fashion Week Daily* site is another place I check out diligently. One section, titled "Daily Media," has all sorts

EXECUTIVE PRODUCERS: TOBY McKEEHAN & JOEY ELWOOD
A&R DIRECTION: JASON S. KING
ART DIRECTION & DESIGN: BOERHAUS.COM
PHOTOGRAPHY: BO STREETER
STYLING: KIM MAXWELL

RECORDED AT THE BORDER (FRANKLIN, TN)

MANAGEMENT:
UNION ENTERTAINMENT / JASON FOWLER / 432.686.8860 / WWW.UEG

BOOKING:
THIRD COAST ARTIST AGENCY / 615.297.2021 / WWW.TCAA.BIZ

THANK YOU:
BONAFIDE: THANKS, EVERYBODY, SERIOUSLY!!!!

MY FIRST OFFICIAL CD CREDIT FROM THE GRITS' CD.

GRITS' REDEMPTION CD COVER. THE FIRST OFFICIAL CD COVER I STYLED.

of articles that discuss the business side of things—who is
retiring, who got promoted, who is starting a new public
relations agency, and which designer line has hired them
for representation. This all-in-one-place site allows me to
keep up with who's working where, in case I need that
information to send over a marketing package or if I'm
looking for a new designer to work with. I also see actress

Liz Hurley has been named the new spokesmodel for Jordache Jeans. I didn't even know they were still working in denim. I used to wear Jordache back in high school, and apparently they're attempting a comeback.

Keja and I arrive at Cumberland Mall at almost the same time. The saleswoman who put the dress on hold for me is off today, and one of the other clerks mistakenly placed it back on the rack. At this point my heart is racing a mile a minute. Here I went to three malls, found the perfect dress for my client—the only one in her size, by the way—and someone returned it to the sales floor. We stand nervously at the register while the sales associate goes out and looks the dress, thankfully finding it after only a few minutes of searching. What makes it so bad is another woman was looking at this dress, too, but she had not yet decided to buy it. We get to it first, so I guess it was destined for Keja to have this dress. She tries it on in the changing room, and it looks beautiful on her. She appears both sexy and classy, which is exactly the look we're going for. It could be a bit tighter around the bust, but that's an easy alteration to make. She wants it hemmed a little higher as well. The dress is backless, which is why I suggested she wear her hair up. The material has a pattern of black, red and bright orange, and I believe gold jewelry and black shoes will look best with it. After making the purchase we walk around the mall in search of accessories, finding the jewelry we want as well as some cute open-toed black platform shoes. Keja is now all set for her New York party. I ask her to have some photos taken so I'll have something for my scrapbook.

MY OFFICE WORK BOARD IS WHERE I POST MY
CALENDAR, THANK-YOU NOTES AND SOME OF
MY FAVORITE THINGS.

I leave Keja at Cumberland Mall around at half-past five to
go home and get ready for an industry event. It's called
Fashion Installation, a terrific get-together that offers people
like me a chance to meet a variety of fashion designers.
Everything gets started at 11:00 P.M., so I have plenty of time
to relax and get ready.

One of the things I like best about working in the fashion
and entertainment industries is that you do your best
networking at various industry parties. I like to party and
I like to network, so it's great to accomplish both at the
same time. This year, Fashion Installation is being held at
The Mark nightclub. Four designers are on display—Pecan
Pie Couture, Redemption Department, Tundrafoot, and Evil
Genius. I like pretty much everything I see and get a chance
to speak with quite a few people in the industry whom I'd
heard of but had not previously met.

LESSONS/PROBLEMS

When I found out that Keja's dress had been returned to the sales rack, I practically had a heart attack. Everything worked out in our favor, since the dress hadn't been sold to someone else. Next time I'll be sure to follow up with the sales associate the day before I go to the store, making sure whatever I've set aside is still put aside.

PREDICTIONS

- *Enjoy my day off*

DIARY

As it's Saturday and I have nothing planned from a work perspective, I decide to sleep in. That's especially welcome since I was out late last night at the fashion event. But even on my "off" days I always begin by checking e-mail, and today I'm glad I did. There's a message from Keshia at Insights Marketing, a copy of one she sent to Mychael, and it's about the swimsuits he designed. It's Super Bowl weekend in Miami where she's promoting the liquor company event, and her message contains some disturbing news. As far as she can tell, the yellow swimsuits did not come out looking the same way they did in Mychael's sketches. I send her a quick response, detailing what I remember about the designs, and she responds almost immediately that the tops appear quite different, and not nearly as nice.

Since she's on the beach, I suggest she might wish to pop into one of the swimwear stores there and buy different tops that she'll like better. I figure it's best if we actually talk about this on the phone, so I call her and we continue our discussion. Keshia explains she noticed the difference as early as Thursday, but Mych never responded to her e-mail. With everything else going on with her promotion, she has no time to go out and buy substitute tops. She also tells me the bottoms don't quite match the sketches either, which I find difficult to understand. I've worked with Mych in the past, and he always delivered exactly what was promised. If I was in Miami today, I explain to Keshia, I'd do the shopping for her. She continues to voice her disappointment and informs me she wants the tops and bottoms corrected and will also expect a partial refund of the price she paid for these swimsuits.

Naturally I apologize for what happened, even though I was the middle person in this project and didn't actually offer the service that was provided. I'm hopeful this problem won't affect any future business projects we do together, and she's quick to assure me that everything is all right between us. As soon as we hang up, I leave a voice-mail message for Mychael that details my conversation with Keshia. I imagine this was nothing more than an oversight on his part, since he's proven himself to be an excellent designer in all the past work we've done together. He continues to be successful in other business ventures other than design. I am sure Keisha and he will come to an agreement and this issue will be resolved.

The day ends with some good news, however. Dionne from the *Get Married* TV program calls to tell me they've confirmed the show's early shooting schedule. She'll e-mail me the details, and I'll call her back if I have any questions.

LESSONS/PROBLEMS
Keshia definitely was not pleased with the yellow swimsuits.

But because I wasn't with her in Miami, there was nothing that I could do about it. Even though I was in the middle, having done little more than facilitate this transaction between two parties, I still felt I needed to do something to make the situation better. Instead of closely examining the sketches and comparing each design to the end-result, all I'd done was look at a couple of suits and assume that everything was correct. Also, if we'd fitted the swimsuits before sending them down to Miami, this problem would have been avoided. The problem was resolved when Mychael and Keshia finally spoke about her issues with the swimsuits and Mychael agreed to resolve the problem by adding straps to the swimsuit bottoms that he had forgotten when he sent them over.

Day 28 | *FEBRUARY 5*

PREDICTIONS
- *Start preparations for the Get Married TV show*
- *Call Dionne to discuss show details*

DIARY

Having learned from Dionne that our TV program will begin taping soon, it's time to start my official show preparations. As promised, all the details are waiting for me in my e-mail inbox. The first message provides me with information on the photo shoots we're doing for the hosts and the production team. At this session—Tuesday, February 20—we'll do headshots of the two stars, Jessica and Jenn, plus their look-book shots. For the "glam" squad, which is comprised of all the people in the makeup, hair and wardrobe department, we're being photographed for the Web site as well. We'll do two different looks, to be depicted in individual headshots as well as a group shot. For one look we're to wear a white outfit, and a black outfit for the other. The glam squad will report at 8:30 A.M. that day, while Jessica's call time is at nine o'clock, and Jenn's at noon.

The second e-mail contains the show's shooting schedule, with all our locations set in Mexico. We'll film three episodes in Cancun on February 11–16. From February 19–21 we'll do episodes in Puerta Vallarta and Los Cabos. Then it's on to Punta Cana for one episode, which will take us from February 26–28 to complete. I have some questions, so I give Dionne a call to discuss them. She wants to do two separate looks each for Jessica and Jenn during their production shoot, and three separate looks once we begin taping the episodes. I'll need to have all wardrobe items pulled no later than the tenth of the month for transport to Mexico, giving us time for everything to clear customs. This schedule is a tight one, and I won't be able to make the trip since I haven't yet received my passport. The production assistant will have to step in and help, although I'm sure I can get the wardrobe items assembled ahead of time to make everyone's job down there go more smoothly.

Once I get off the phone with Dionne, I pick up a voice-mail message from Jessica. The show's producer has told her she'll need two swimsuits for the Mexico shoots. I hadn't planned on pulling swimwear for this show, so now I have to find a company that's willing to act as the sponsor for these items. I decide to start by visiting two local stores I've seen that carry women's beach attire, introduce myself to store management, and try to talk them into providing suits for our show. After filling Dionne and Jessica in on my plans, I call Lakeisha to set up a prep meeting for *Get Married.* We'll get together tomorrow evening to discuss whatever plans need to be made.

Now it's time for some serious shopping. My first stop is Atlanta Beach. I've passed by this place many times in the past but have never stopped in. They have a reputation for some really cute swimsuits, and I've also noticed their billboards around town. I walk through the store to get a basic feeling for their selection, and I see a number of designs worth further examination. This store has on display many different colors and styles in designer-name swimsuits. I introduce myself to one of the sales associates, and she explains the owner of the store won't be in until tomorrow. I'm invited to write down my name and what I have in mind. After leaving her with one of my business cards, I also make sure to obtain the owner's contact information so I can follow up with her tomorrow. Time is short, which means I don't have time to wait for someone to call me back.

The next swimwear store on my agenda is Swim 'n' Sport in Lenox Square Mall. It's immediately apparent that this place carries some truly hot swimwear. I introduce myself to the store manager and her assistant, and they're excited about the possibility of us using their swimwear on television. The store manager offers me the phone number to their corporate office, where the marketing department will need to make the decision on sponsorship. I step outside the store and give that number a call, reaching the administrative assistant for the corporation. She provides me with the name of the company president and explains that I'll need to put me request in writing. I make note of the fax number so there will be no delay in sending over the appropriate paperwork, since timing is critical.

Tomorrow I'll check out the Swim 'n' Sport Web site and compose my two letters of request. Even though I saw some really cute suits at the Atlanta Beach store, I have a feeling Swim 'n' Sport will be the swimwear company we'll use. Everyone there was very nice to me, and they seemed excited with the business opportunity presented to them.

LESSONS/PROBLEMS

This job often forces me to think quickly on my feet. Only
today did I learn I'd have to pull swimwear for the *Get
Married* TV program. Fortunately I'm always on the lookout
for clothing sources, and I remembered two stores that
would likely have what I needed. Everyone was helpful and
friendly, which always makes my job easier.

PREDICTIONS

* *Research two swimwear suppliers*
* *Create a stylist request letter*
* *Meet with Lakeisha to discuss Get Married*

DIARY

I start my day online by doing research on the swimwear companies I'd like to see sponsor our TV show. I prefer to familiarize myself with a company's product line before composing a stylist request letter. Atlanta Beach doesn't appear to have a Web presence, but I do find one for Swim 'n' Sport. The company is based in Florida and has 34 locations in 12 states. Most of their swim line is depicted online, and everything I see looks terrific. I'm convinced their designs will go well with the image I'm trying to build for Jessica.

There are certain things I'm always sure to mention when writing a stylist request letter. I start with my name and my role with *Get Married*. Then I explain the program's concept and mention the shooting dates, the dates it will air, and the show's Web address. I also provide details on Women's Entertainment Television, the network that's broadcasting the show, and describe the benefits of getting free advertisement on *Get Married* if they decide to sponsor the swimsuits. It offers them a ton of free advertising, and what company doesn't like that? It's especially valuable when the show happens to target the very demographic market they're aiming for. At the end of the letter I list the number of swimsuits I'd like to borrow and the dates I want to pull them. After both letters are printed and signed, I fax them to their respective owners. Finally, I follow up with a phone call to make sure everything is received. Now we'll see which company responds first, and who will give us the best offer.

Several hours later I receive a phone call from Sherri, who represents Swim 'n' Sport. She tells me the company president is definitely interested in working with us. They're willing to sponsor two swimsuits for our first episode, and I'm welcome to pull additional outfits whenever we tape in another exotic location. I make sure to thank her profusely and then ask if I can stop by their Lenox Square location on February 9 to pull the swimwear. She offers to contact the store manager and let her know I'll be coming in. My next call is to Jessica. We arrange to meet at the mall on the ninth for a fitting session. I also contact the store manager there to let her know we'll be in around 3: 30 P.M. that day. Finally I send Dionne a text message and give her all the details on the sponsorship and the upcoming fitting. I find that it's best to let everyone know what's going on as soon as it's arranged. That way, there are no surprises.

Lakeisha arrives at six o'clock, and we sit down together to review all the material I've included in the *Get Married* file folder. I inform her we'll start pulling wardrobe items on February 9, beginning with Fabrik at noon and then Swim 'n' Sport at half past three. There are other dates to discuss as well. A photo shoot is scheduled for February 20, so we'll need to pull two looks each for Jessica and Jenn. Each of us will need two separate looks for our own pictures as well. We'll pull the clothes the day before the shoot. Then Lakeisha and I look over Jessica and Jenn's client folders so we can familiarize ourselves with their individual styles. We also go through the notes taken at the first pre-production meeting we had with the glam squad and the production crew.

LESSONS/PROBLEMS

Everything worked out well today, since I managed to nail down a swimsuit sponsor for our television show on very short notice. Everything seems to be falling into place on this project.

DISCUSSING WARDROBE TERMS AND AGREEMENTS WITH FABRIK BOUTIQUE'S MANAGER.

Day 30 | *FEBRUARY 9*

PREDICTIONS

- *Pull wardrobe items at Fabrik*
- *Fitting with Jessica at Swim 'n' Sport*

DIARY

At ten o'clock I call Fabrik to remind them we'll be in at noon to pull wardrobe for *Get Married*. I ring up Swim 'n' Sport and give them the same message. Both store managers confirm our visits. I also check with Lakeisha to make sure she'll be there to give me a hand. Then I gather up all the paperwork I'll need to bring with me—client folders, the *Get Married* folder, and a login sheet to keep track of the wardrobe items we'll be pulling from each of the two stores.

I get to Fabrik on time and discuss exactly which outfits we'll be pulling and when they should expect them returned with the store manager. After that, Lakeisha and I go over the client folders and start looking for wardrobe items. As we set aside the outfits we'll take with us, Dionne calls to tell me the shooting dates have been delayed because the producer has come down with pneumonia. We'll still do our prep work for the glam squad photo shoot, but the departure has been changed to February 18. We immediately stop pulling wardrobe here, since we're not planning to use it right away.

We get to the Swim 'n' Sport store around two o'clock, even though our fitting with Jessica is not for another ninety minutes. We pick out swimsuits we think would look great on Jessica and put them in the dressing room. Then we walk around the mall to kill time, at which point Jessica calls to tell me she's stuck in traffic. It must have been a pretty bad jam, because she shows up a full hour late. I've only arranged for Lakeisha to work with me until 4:30 P.M. but she agrees to stay and help me out, which is why I value her so much as an assistant. When Jessica gets to her dressing room, I present her with six swimsuits we've pulled. After trying each one on, we decide on the two best-looking ones and I take photographs of her in them for my client file. Then we fill out the necessary paperwork with the store manager before leaving around six o'clock.

LESSONS/PROBLEMS
All week I'd planned carefully to pull the wardrobe needed for the *Get Married* TV show. At the last minute I learned the

AT SWIM 'N SPORT DISCUSSING SWIMSUIT OPTIONS WITH JESSICA, THE HOST OF GET MARRIED TV.

MY ASSISTANT, LAKEISHA LOOKING FOR ACCESSORIES AT FABRIK FOR THE GET MARRIED TV SHOW.

travel schedule was delayed. Since we don't need the outfits right away, it didn't make sense to pull them. Because delays like this happen all the time, I wasn't upset and simply rolled with the punches. I'll hold onto my paperwork and come back in a week to pull the items for the show.

KEY TERMS

ARTIST INFORMATION SHEET
Listing of an artist's music information and project details.

ASSISTANT
Someone who helps the stylist with preparing, working, and wrapping up a project.

BLING
Flashy and expensive jewelry.

BOOKING AGENT
Individual who represents a stylist by booking jobs and negotiating deals.

COMP CARD
Card that contains photo samples of your work.

CONFIRMATION AGREEMENT
Written document that confirms the agreed terms, rates, and dates of a project.

CLIENT SHEET
Listing of a client's contact details and clothing sizes.

DAY RATE
Amount of money a stylist is paid per eight-hour day to work on a project.

IMAGE
How a person wants to be perceived in the public eye.

LOGIN SHEET
Document that keeps track of wardrobe items pulled from a showroom or boutique.

LOOK BOOK
Book that shows different looks of a designer's collection.

PERSONAL STYLE
How an individual prefers to dress.

PREP
To prepare for a project by consulting with a client, pulling wardrobe items, fitting the client for the wardrobe, etc.

PUBLICIST
Professional who is intimately familiar with the tools and techniques of getting exposure for clients on a regional, national, or international basis.

PULL
Selecting wardrobe items to rent from a showroom, boutique or department store.

TEARSHEET COLLECTION SHEET
Listing of tearsheets or photos a stylist needs to collect from a client.

STYLIST LETTER
Correspondence from a stylist to various suppliers that requests the rental or purchase of various wardrobe items.

STYLIST KIT
Items a stylist carries to a project to help create an image—may contain tape, shoe polish, needle and thread, pens, lint brush, scissors, etc.

TEARSHEET
Sample one's work that has been published in a magazine and subsequently torn out.

TREND REPORT
Report that explains fashion trends for the current or upcoming season.

WARDROBE RENTAL AGREEMENT
Formal agreement between a stylist and a supplier that lists the terms, fees and dates of rented wardrobe items.

WARDROBE CONTACT BOOK
Book that contains business cards of businesses that supply wardrobe items.

WRAP
To finish up a project by retagging wardrobe items and returning them to the supplier.